The Monk Who Became Chief Minister

The Monk Who Became Chief Minister

The Definitive Biography of Yogi Adityanath

Shantanu Gupta

B L O O M S B U R Y
NEW DELHI • LONDON • OXFORD • NEW YORK • SYDNEY

BLOOMSBURY INDIA
Bloomsbury Publishing India Pvt. Ltd
Second Floor, LSC Building No. 4, DDA Complex,
Pocket C – 6 & 7, Vasant Kunj,
New Delhi 110070

BLOOMSBURY and the Diana logo are trademarks of
Bloomsbury Publishing Plc

First published in India 2017
This edition published 2025

ISBN: 978-93-86606-42-6
2 4 6 8 10 9 7 5 3

Typeset by Manipal Digital Systems
Printed and bound in India by Gopsons Papers Pvt. Ltd, Noida

MIX
Paper | Supporting responsible forestry
FSC® C191020

Contents

Foreword

Yoga is the defining term for India and its great dharmic civilization of thousands of years. The global spread of Yoga since Swami Vivekananda first travelled to the West over a hundred years ago has paralleled India's development as a nation.

In March 2017 Yogi Adityanath, head of the eminent Gorakhdham Mutt, became the Chief Minister of Uttar Pradesh, the most populous state in India. His appointment, which was a great surprise to many, marks a significant new chapter in the ongoing relationship between Yoga and India's national awakening.

The current Prime Minister of India Sri Narendra Modi, with his establishment of International Yoga Day and bringing Yoga education into the schools, has emphasized this connection. By selecting Yogi Adityanath, the BJP that Modi leads has furthered this yogic vision of a new India. Yogic values and practices can help us better perform our duties and create a happier, more prosperous and aware society. This is particularly relevant and possible in India, the land of Yoga.

Gorakhdham Mutt is one of the most prestigious seats of yogic knowledge in the country. Yogi Gorakhnath, who the Mutt represents, has been the most influential of India's Yogis over many centuries. He was a famous exponent of Hatha Yoga and its psychophysical exercises and of Siddha Yoga and its deep meditation practices.

As representing Gorakhdham Mutt, Yogi Adityanath carries on this venerable tradition of Nath Yoga, which long ago spread throughout South Asia bringing the light of Yoga to the entire region. As a Nath Yogi, Adityanath has a training and a heritage perhaps unparalleled among political figures today.

Nath Yogis are Hindu Shaivites, but in the universal view of Shaivism and Sanatana Dharma, share their teachings for the benefit of all peoples, regardless of religious or cultural backgrounds. They follow strict vows and practices aimed at both inner spiritual awakening and providing service to humanity. Historically, Nath Yogis served in the protection of temples and holy sites.

While Yogi Adityanath is the first Yogi to become a chief minister in India, we must remember that great Yogis like Sri Aurobindo played crucial roles in India's Independence Movement. The *Bhagavad Gita* of Yogeshvara Krishna inspired the movement overall and remains India's most characteristic and widely read book.

Yogi Adityanath received his initiation in 1994 from revered Mahant Avaidyanath, the head of Gorakhnath Mutt and disciple of famous Mahant Digvijaynath. He became head of the Mutt himself in 2014 when Avaidyanath passed away.

Yogi Adityanath contested and became a member of the Lok Sabha from Gorakhpur in 1998, at the age of 26; the youngest person ever elected to the Lok Sabha, and has not lost an election since. He took over the seat from his own guru Mahant Avaidyanath who had previously held it for many years, working for the country according to the same yogic values. His Mutt has many upliftment programs for all segments of society, including women, the youth and the poor.

Yogi Adityanath has not only a vast spiritual heritage but also the extensive government experience necessary to run such a large state as UP, taking an active role in Lok Sabha functions and committees over the years. He conducts regular Janta Darbars for meeting with the common people and discussing their problems on all levels. Yogi Adityanath reflects yogic attitudes and values in his working to improve education, increase infrastructure, and counter crime and corruption.

With such extraordinary accomplishments already, Yogi Adityanath at the young age of forty-four is a leader with a destiny likely to remain a key figure in India for decades to come. Sri Narendra Modi's commitment both to India's development and to promoting Yoga is part of the Yogi's inspiration.

Uttar Pradesh has over two hundred million people, more populous than but a few countries in the world. Sadly the state has suffered from decades of misrule and lack of development, including massive corruption under previous administrations. Though Uttar Pradesh is the ancient center of India culturally, misrule and nepotism has kept it one of the most backward regions of the country. This makes uplifting the state a daunting challenge requiring a leader of Yogi Adityanath's stature and determination. Given his special background, it is imperative that people today learn more about Yogi Adityanath and what he truly represents.

Shantanu Gupta recently wrote *Compilation of Prime Minister's Mann Ki Baat*, explaining with clarity and depth the thoughts and guidance of PM Narendra Modi from his weekly radio addresses. In *The Monk Who Became Chief Minister*, he has provided a detailed analysis of the life of Yogi Adityanath – a well-informed biography of the Yogi's personal, public and spiritual aspects, particularly relative to his recent election.

Readers will find it fascinating to delve into the story of this young and transformative leader of the new India. The book brings the Yogi alive and allows us to understand his key ideas and statements, and appreciate his strong character and determination.

The Monk Who Became Chief Minister is well researched and referenced, replete with extensive factual data and illuminating comments. It covers all aspects of the Yogi's work, including the controversies that have been created around him. It is likely to be an authoritative study for years to come.

It is true that some groups, particularly the far left in India, will remain suspicious of Yogi Adityanath whatever he does, much as they have long opposed Narendra Modi. This opposition extends to a few western publications that continue negative colonial narratives about India. Given such potential distortions, the book provides a balanced view of the Yogi that can counter any misinformation.

Today a new world is dawning in the high tech era and with it a new India in what could be called the "post-Nehruvian post-Marxist era". India under the new vision of PM Modi is now the fastest developing economy in the world and one of the most influential countries in global diplomacy and international relations. Uniquely, India preserves the oldest spiritual traditions of humanity as well promoting the new knowledge and expertise that science and information technology provides – a rare combination that Yogi Adityanath endorses.

Yogi Adityanath is a national and world leader for the future. He represents India's new aspirational generation that aims to develop the country without abandoning its profound civilizational ethos. Let us follow carefully what his guidance brings. He may surprise his critics, uplifting the state and the country by demonstrating a new model of yogic leadership to the world.

Dr. David Frawley (Vamadeva Shastri)
Padma Bhushan Awardee and Founder,
American Institute of Vedic Studies

Preface

On 19 March 2017, Yogi Adityanath took an oath as the twenty first Chief Minister of Uttar Pradesh. You may know a few things about him, you may have seen some media coverage and might have read some stories; some biased, some exaggerated and some real. But there is much more that makes Yogi Adityanath.

This biography takes you through four facets of Yogi Adityanath's life in its four sections. The book starts with Yogi's current avatar, as Chief Minister of Uttar Pradesh, electoral politics of 2017 Uttar Pradesh assembly elections, dynamics behind Yogi's selection as the CM of UP and initial days of Yogi at the *Pancham Tal* (CM Office of UP). The second section takes you through the life of this long standing, five-time parliamentarian Yogi Adityanath, his electoral victories, his meticulous interventions in parliament, the truth behind his so-called controversial speeches, the rationale behind his idea of love-jihad, re-conversion, Hindu Yuva Vahini and his relationship with the BJP. In the third section I take my readers through the life of Mahant of Gorakhnath mutt, Yogi Adityanath, his rigorous yogic routine, about gurus of *Nath Panth*, and socio-political activities of the mutt over the decades. In last section I will leave my readers with some very engaging first-hand accounts of the upbringing of a young boy Ajay Singh Bisht, in the hinterlands of Uttarakhand, who grew up among cows, farms, mountains and rivers to later become a Mahant, a Parliamentarian and the Chief Minister.

Through extensive research I have accumulated unseen pictures, unheard instances, first-time interviews, with people close to Yogi, in this biography. The book takes you through the journey of a shy and introvert boy from the hills of Uttarakhand, who had a modern education in the faculties of science from Kotdwar, later took *sanyas* and went through rigorous training in *vedic* education. From being a rebel politician inside and outside the party, he now has become a man of consensus. This book explores how a *Nath Panthi* monk, learnt the nuances of politics from his guru, Mahant Awaidnath, and rose to take the highest position in Uttar Pradesh's politics. A state with 22 crore people and 80 Lok Sabha seats, is one of the very crucial political pieces in India's electoral puzzle. With a history of producing many Prime Ministers for the country, the State has given yet another prospect for the Prime Minister's office, in the post-Modi era in the form of Yogi Adityanath. You have in your hands the first definitive biography of a monk who has become the Chief Minister of the most populous state of India.

While writing this biography, I spent time in Gorakhnath Mutt, learning about *Nath Panth*, originating from *Mahayogi* Adinath Lord Shiva, learning how Guru Matsyendranātha, and Guru Goraksanātha structured the teachings of *Nath Panth*, I also discovered the various rituals and symbols of *nath panth*, the tenants of Hath Yoga and, it gave me goose bumps to realize that I am standing on such hallowed grounds. A place where once, Guru Goraksanātha practiced and taught yoga, where hundreds of *Nath Panth* yogis gathered on various auspicious occasions, where in modern times *'ram janmbhoomi'* movement deliberations were conducted, a Mutt which was always socially and politically active and its mahants represented the region in State Assembly and National Parliament and the Mutt which gave a *Nath Panthi yogi*, a *kanphata sadhu* as the twenty first Chief Minister of Uttar Pradesh. I feel this State is blessed to have a descendent and disciple of Adinath Lord Shiva, to serve its 22 crore people and I am also equally blessed to be able to bring the story of this monk to my readers.

Shantanu Gupta

Acknowledgements

Many people deserve my sincerest thanks for assisting me in bringing the story of Yogi Adityanath to my readers. I would like to express heartfelt appreciation to everyone who I have come in contact with, through the course of completing this book. I will mention a few names that stand out, without whom this would not have been possible.

Firstly I would like to thank Savita Devi Ji, Anand Singh Bisht Ji, Deepak Chandra, Dr Umesh Tyagi, who spent long hours with me narrating Yogi's childhood stories and giving me an insight into the life of the charismatic leader we all know today.

Padmesh Budlakoti, Akash Rawat, Neeraj Agarwal, Babita Rana and Anil Bisht, who spent time with me to talk about Yogi's Kotdwar days and give us a glimpse of Yogi's life as a young man clearly destined for greater things.

Teachers at Bharat Mandir Intercollege, Bansi Dhar Pokhriyal, DPS Rawat, Devendra Kumar Varshney and Yogi's classmate Ajay Bisht have my deepest gratitude for telling me all the stories from Yogi Adityanath's schooling in Rishikesh. Ravi Prakash needs a special mention for connecting me with the teachers at Bharat Mandir Inter College.

Dwarka Nath Tiwari, Pradeep Rao, PK Mal, Arunesh Shahi, all the Saints and Volunteers at the Mutt for helping me know about Yogi's life after taking *sanyas*. Raj Bhushan Singh Rawat for connecting us with all the people close to Yogi Adityanath. I am grateful to the computer operator of the Gorakhnath Mutt, Vinay Kumar Gautam, for helping us with the rare photographs of Yogi Adityanath.

Thanks to Akshay Kumar Singh and Pradeep Sharma for assisting me with the online research for the book.

Swapnika Duggu and Megha Mukherjee, thanks to you for copy editing the book for me. I am immensely thankful to have friends like Sandeep Deo and Rajiv Tiwari who gave honest feedback and great advice at various stages. I am very grateful to my publisher Praveen Tiwari, from Bloombury India, who has assisted me in bringing this book to my readers. Syed Dilshad Ali deserves acknowledgement for coming up with the amazing cover for the book and Vaibhav Gupta for taking all the photographs and interview videos during my research travel. Satendra Singh and Puskar Sharma have been a great source of support and have helped me in all the logistics for the research for the biography.

Most importantly I have to thank my wife Swetha Rao Duggu and my son Abhiram who allowed me to keep my focus and have motivated me to complete this book on time and for also putting up with my erratic schedule and travel without ever complaining. Finally I'd like to add that all of this also would not have been possible without the prayers and blessings of my parents and rest of my family who have always believed in me.

Section 1.
Yogi Adityanath, Chief Minister of Uttar Pradesh

Yogi Adityanath took oath as 21st Chief Minister of UP

"I, Adiyanath Yogi do swear in the name of God/solemnly affirm that I will bear true faith and allegiance to the Constitution of India as by law established, that I will uphold the sovereignty and integrity of India, that I will faithfully and conscientiously discharge my duties as a Chief Minister for the State of Uttar Pradesh and that I will do right to all manner of people in accordance with the Constitution and the law without fear or favour, affection or ill-will. I do swear in the name of God/solemnly affirm that I will not directly or indirectly communicate or reveal to any person or persons any matter which shall be brought under my consideration or shall become known to me as a Chief Minister for the State of Uttar Pradesh except as may be required for the due discharge of my duties as Chief Minister..."

Just before the oath, the Master of Ceremony announced – "We formally start the oath taking ceremony with the permission of the Honorable Governor. Honorable Governor has appointed Yogi Adityanath ji as the Chief Minister of Uttar Pradesh." With this declaration, the crowd erupted into a frenzy and Yogi Adityanath stood and greeted everyone with folded hands.

After the oath, amid the cheering by the *karyakartas* (party volunteers), Yogi first greeted the Governor, then Prime Minister Modi, followed by party president Amit Shah, senior leaders Rajnath Singh, Lal Krishna Advani, Murali Manohar Joshi, Venkaiah Naidu, other Chief Ministers and senior leaders of BJP and the National Democratic Alliance (NDA). As Yogi walked around the stage with humility and confidence, the nation has observed a new mass leader in the making. By now political pundits had already started visualizing, tweeting and writing about Yogi as the future Prime Minister of India.

Why BJP chose Yogi for the CM post?

After a fiercely fought UP elections and a huge win in 2017, it was not easy for Bhartiya Janta Party (BJP) to select the head of this newly won State. Media was throwing various names every hour. Rajnath Singh, Yogi Adityanath, Uma Bharti, Manoj Sinha, Swatantra Dev Singh, Dinesh Sharma, Keshav Prasad Maurya, Varun Gandhi, Satish Mahana, Suresh Khanna and many more. There are various theories, floating around on how BJP nailed down on Yogi's name for the highest post of the most populous state of the country. Most of these theories are based on the traditional regional, political and caste-wise calculations, like, which castes had voted for BJP, who was close to Rashtriya Swamsevak Sangh (RSS), who was close to the Gujarati duo of Prime Minister and Party President etc. For a popular mandate like this, the BJP seems to have wanted to appoint an equally popular leader as the CM of UP. On the day when PM Narendra Modi, addressed the party workers at the party national headquarters after the success of 2017 Assembly elections in five states, he declared that this is a mandate for a new India. Rajnath Singh and Uma Bharti are now old guards. Varun Gandhi, never toed the party line and ran a parallel campaign, which had already antagonized the senior leadership in the past. Finally, the needle stopped at Yogi Adityanath. In a recent interview on a Hindi channel, AajTak, Yogi said that he has given his passport to PMO for approval for a high-level Parliamentary committee foreign tour. The PMO advised him not to go out of the country in light of the upcoming UP results. He was not too happy about the PMO's decision, but he did not know then, that something bigger was waiting for him.

Does the 44-year-old Yogi fit the bill of #IAmNewIndia (a phrase coined by the PM) over the other seasoned leaders? What we know of Yogi through the media is that he is 'A Hindu Hardliner'. Front pages of leading newspapers greeted Yogi's anointment as the Chief Minister of Uttar Pradesh with colored headlines, – 'A Hindu Priest as Chief Minister,' An RSS backed Chief Minister, 'A Chief Minister for the Ram-Mandir Mission' and many such stereotypical headlines. Scanning through his record as a Parliamentarian, the questions he raised in the Parliament, the debates he participated in, and my interaction with people at the Janta Darbar of Gorakhnath Mutt, gave me a very different picture. I have discovered that he has been a very rigorous Parliamentarian over last two decades, both in Lok Sabha and in his constituency. From the time of Mahant Avaidyanath, the mutt has provided a grievance redressal system, in the form of *Janta Darbars*, for resolving citizens' issues with the local administration. Locals say that a letter from the Mutt, means that your work will be done, even in a State that is non-BJP. Pradeep Rao, who handles various institutions for the mutt and a close aide of Yogi Adityanath, fondly recollects that Mahant Avaidyanath used to request the local administration to help the needy, but could be convinced to stop Mutt's persuasions of a particular case, if local officials show their inability to close the matter, due to administrative bottlenecks. Rao adds that with Yogi Adityanath is it a different case. For any genuine issue, he first calls the required official and sends a letter to the officer and if that doesn't work, he displays a show of strength, in form of a non-violent protest, with a large group of volunteers in front of officials' work place or camp office.

Overtime officials realised that, it is better to listen to the phone calls and letters, rather than waiting for Yogi's cavalcade and supporters to storm into their office.

Yogi's escalation as the Chief Minister of Uttar Pradesh is also significant in BJP's overall polity. Grooming popular local leaders has worked for BJP in the last four decades. Modi's rise in the party itself was meteoric as he became the PM candidate for 2014 elections over BJP veterans like Lal Krishna Advani, Murali Manohar Joshi and the natural leaders in both houses of Parliament – Sushma Swaraj and Arun Jaitley. One should give credit to BJP and its inherent structure, which allows strong local leaders to take center stage, whenever the opportunity arises. Comparing this with Congress gives a completely different picture. After the 'Strong Center and Committed bureaucracy' formula adopted by Indira Gandhi, no one in the Congress found the mettle and courage to reverse it. Over decades Congress humiliated and ignored the strong local leaders, which lead to multiple vertical splits and exits from the party. Sharad Pawar, Mamata Banerjee, Biju Patnaik, Jagan Reddy and many such names, left Congress as they were not given their due in the party.

Yogi is extremely popular among youth, and BJP voters, which is evident in numerous fan pages and campaigns being run for him on various digital platforms. Added to this, Yogi is a five-time parliamentarian, with amazing parliamentary performance in debates, questions and private member bills. He has had modern and *vedic* education and the experience of handling large scale institutions of Gorakhnath mutt and making him the Chief Minister of UP, seems completely inline with BJP's philosophy of escalating strong and popular local leaders to the highest position.

However the national and international media is unable to digest the escalation of a saffron clad leader to the post of Chief Minister of the most populous state of India. Market of conspiracy theories is ripe. Catch News tried to float a theory that Yogi was appointed as the CM of Uttar Pradesh by RSS against the will of Modi and Amit Shah. They published a report on 27 May, 2017 that – "The most significant part of what looks like a serious face-off between Adityanath and Modi is that the RSS is reportedly backing the CM. There is a sense in the Sangh that Yogi's presence as UP CM helps achieve the ideological consolidation they want. Many observers have also said that appointment of the mahant from Gorakhpur as UP CM fits in perfectly with the RSS' plans to openly espouse majoritarianism for its next stage of political expansion. From the point of view of Modi and Amit Shah, Adityanath is a clear deviation from the script. Till now all the chief ministers they had appointed were low key leaders or those from a strong RSS background – Manohar Lal Khattar and Raghubar Das being cases in point. Also, many of the CMs are from numerically weak communities in their respective states. Khattar is a Khatri in Jat dominated Haryana, Jharkhand CM Raghubar Das is the non-tribal CM in Jharkhand, Devendra Fadnavis is only the second Brahmin CM in Maratha dominated Maharashtra, Sarbananda Sonowal is from an ethnic minority community in Assam and Gujarat CM Vijay Rupani is a Jain. Adityanath is a deviation on both counts as he has considerable mass following and he also belongs to the powerful Thakur community. Given these factors and the RSS backing, it is clear that Adityanath is fast becoming a power center, something that is cause of concern for Modi and Shah".

Reality of the situation is that Modi and Shah were looking for a popular and a strong face and got that combination in Yogi Adityanath. Amit Shah was already quite impressed with Yogi Adityanath's strong presence on the ground. In 2013, Amit Shah was sent to Uttar Pradesh as the in-charge for UP in the run up to the 2014 Lok Sabha elections. Amit Shah travelled widely to understand the dynamics and demography of UP and while traveling through Gorakhpur, he faced violent opposition from the locals[1]. He did not have any security that time with him. He called Yogi Adityanath

1 http://www.jansatta.com/national/who-chose-yogi-adityanath-as-up-cm-in-mutually-contradictory-claims-ndtv-political-editor-says-he-was-amit-shah-choice/281494/

and within no time, many young volunteers of Hindu Yuva Vahini, came on bikes and cleared the way for Amit Shah.

A section of the media alleges that Yogi and the mutt also have a history of pressurizing BJP for tickets for candidates from Hindu Yuva Vahini. In Gorakhpur, this is common anecdote that in 2002, Yogi had put a candidate, Dr. Radha Mohan Das Agarwal against Shiv Pratap Shukla of BJP under the Hindu Mahasabha and campaigned openly for him and in fact Dr. Agarwal won that election. Later Yogi made Dr. Agarwal join BJP and in 2007, 2012 & 2017 Dr. Agarwal won this seat on BJP's ticket, keeping Shiv Pratap Shukla away from Gorakhpur's electoral politics.

In 2017 BJP was far more coherent compared to the previous three assembly electoral battles. In 2017, all the forces joined and Yogi was made one of the star campaigners by the party. After initial resistance, Yogi cooperated with the party, for ticket distribution and infact sacked Sunil Singh, state head and Ram Laxman, General Secretary of *Hindu Yuva Vahini* (HYV), for indiscipline. 2017 was a fiercely fought tri-polar election, where file and rank of the BJP and like-minded cultural groups came along to uproot the decade and a half long rule of regional parties.

Uttar Pradesh Assembly Elections, 2017

BJP knew that, the party performed poorly in Uttar Pradesh in last three assembly elections. After 2014's fabulous win, the party did not sit back on their laurels. Amit Shah has put one of his best men, Sunil Bansal, in charge for BJP's organizational rejuvenation in the state. As organizational General Secretary of BJP, UP, Bansal started tying up the loose ends of the BJP at the booth level. Bansal with his strong organizational skills of ABVP days, backed by his equally strong information technology team of IITians, went from strength to strength through membership drive, *sampark*(contact) drive, training drive, flag march drive, *parivartan yatra*(change drive), *kamal mela*(lotus fest) and many more such well-designed organizational strengthening drives. Bansal and his team were able to identify new position holders at state, district, mandal and booth level. Through all these drives BJP was able to highlight the inefficiencies and blatant corruption of the BSP & SP regimes to the masses. Coupled with this, the organizational back up by Rashtriya Swam Sevak Sangh (RSS), long standing political experience of state coordinator, Om Mathur, meticulous planning of Prime Minister's grand rallies by state general secretary Swatantra Dev Singh and charming face of OBC leader and party State President Keshav Prasad Maurya, worked in party's favor.

With a mass strength of 22 crores, only five countries in the world can match Uttar Pradesh's population. With 80 Lok Sabha seats and a history of producing the highest number of Prime Ministers, UP's electoral dynamics is a feast for politicians & election pundits. Results for this fiercely fought 2017 UP assembly elections came on 11 March. Bhartiya Janta Party (BJP) and his allies swept the state of Uttar Pradesh with 325 seats out of 403 seats in the State Assembly, clinching almost 42 percent of the vote share.

Barring *chanakya*, none of the exit poles came close to this verdict. Most of the political pundits and psephologists look clueless to provide a sensible theory behind this victory. All of them are trained to theorize political campaigns and victories based on some arithmetic of caste, religion, age, gender and region. The voting pattern, defied all such traditional patterns & logics. BJP's Brijesh Singh, won the Deoband seat, which is known for its famous Darul Uloom, Islamic school. Congress dominated, Amethi seat is won by BJP's Garima Singh. This undefined wave has successfully stormed Amethi and Raebareli, the long-standing bastions of the Nehru-Gandhi family. The Yadav family *bahu* (bride), Aparna Yadav lost her seat from Lucknow. Bundelkhand region, usually dominated by SP & BSP, is wiped out by BJP. Political pundits said that Jats of west UP are angry with BJP, because of the reservation issue of Haryana, but they seemed to have voted for BJP in the west.

With merely 19 seats in UP 2017 Assembly elections, Bahujan Samaj Party (BSP) will struggle for even a single Rajya Sabha seat. Irritated of losing her base, Mayavati has blamed it on Electronic Voting Machines (EVMs). Congress's P. Chidambaram, National Conference's Umar Abdulla, have conceded to the Narendra Modi wave. Some say its Hindu consolidation, some say Mayawati lost money in demonetization and was not able to campaign properly and leaders of Samajvadi party started murmuring that alliance with Congress has caused them this humiliating defeat. To all the pundits, psephologists, analysts, surveyors, social scientists, political scientists and journalists, I say – stop the traditional age old parochial analysis based on caste, religion, gender and region, wake up to new India, which is voting for aspirations, development and to the idea of a powerful India.

Many did not notice, but this change in electoral discourse started in 2014. 2014 Lok Sabha elections were different in many ways. Apart from a historically decisive mandate for Bhartiya Janta Party (BJP) lead coalition, the positive campaign of Narendra Modi, focused on development and governance, changed the grammar of political campaigning in India forever. Adding to this, Anna Hazare and Baba Ramdev's movements sharpened the discourse of anti-corruption in the country. For the first time someone boldly attempted to communicate the language of aspiration versus the language of victimization, which was the trend of electoral messaging till then. So much so that Modi's doctrine of 'Minimum Government, Maximum Governance', 'Per Drop More Crop', 'Government has No Business to be in Business', 'Tourism Unites, Terrorism Divides' and 14 such themes took the shape of 'Moditva' compilation, which was more talked about than the party's official manifesto.

This phenomenon has made it compulsory for all political parties battling in the *kurukshetra* of Uttar Pradesh assembly elections 2017, to have a component of development and aspirations in their electoral syllabus. Modi led BJP came up with a very comprehensive strategy for the state of Uttar Pradesh, in the form of '*Lok Kalyan Sankalp Patra*' (People's welfare charter). Some also say, that Yogi as a CM choice was evident in the party's electoral campaign. Themes in BJP's Lok Kalyan Sankalp Patra, like banning illegal slaughterhouses, anti-Romeo squad, etc. were common in Yogi's narrative for many years. Also Yogi was extensively used for campaigning through out the state. Samajvadi Party (SP) had to devise a family dispute, to help Akhilesh come out as a clean leader, with '*Kam Bolta Hai*' (Work Speaks) punch line. Even Congress has harped on the '*27 Saal UP Behal*' (UP in bad shape for last 27 years) campaign to point out the failures of previous governments. Though their electoral opportunism, made Congress shake hands with SP, which they were opposing vehemently until as late as January 2017. Irony laughed loudly during the joint road show of Rahul Gandhi and Akhilesh Yadav, when they were both captured entangled in hanging electrical wires, while chanting 'Kam Bolta Hai'. Far from all these narratives, Mayawati still seemed to don her old strategy of social engineering, caste calculations and securing *dalit-brahmin* and *dalit-muslim* equations. Apart from reminding people of her marginally better law and order record, she did not seem to have much to offer in her speeches.

So it's clear that the current Prime Minister has altered the rules of electoral battles. He looks very confident in the new rules, as he has a long three-term experience of governance and bringing real change in Gujarat, especially in implementing ease of doing business policy, constant power supply and a world-class public infrastructure. His two and a half years of tenure in center also got a very positive reception from the ground. After a long time, people observed a Prime Minister, who is able to communicate with people and to convince them to keep India clean, is able to convince people to give up their subsidies and is also able to get people to stand in queues for hours to kill the menace of unaccounted money. For the people of Uttar Pradesh, the vocabulary of development is rather new. Akhilesh, Mayawati and Rahul attempted this new vocabulary, but failed as their limping track records did not walk the talk.

In my previous book '*Uttar Pradesh – Vikas ki Pratiksha mein*[2]' (Uttar Pradesh is waiting for development) I clinically

---

2 *Uttar Pradesh – 'Vikas ki Pratiksha mein'*, by Shantanu Gupta, Publisher: Bloomsbury, India

examined the electoral development promises of governments in UP in last 15 years. This book touched upon the historical, cultural and social backdrop of Uttar Pradesh and explored the current and past political scenario emerging in UP. I focused on the point that, even though UP is very important politically, development still eludes UP. Even today the state is struggling with poor electricity, bad roads, pathetic law and order, poor education and low rankings in ease of doing business; all resulting in lack of employment for the youth. Here, I am drawing upon some research done for my previous book, to understand the results of UP assembly elections of 2017, which gave us Yogi Adityanath as the Chief Minister of the state.

UP contributes 16.5 percent to the population of India, but only 8.5 percent to its GDP. If we compare this data to Gujarat, that contributes 5 percent to India's population and 7.5 percent to its GDP. This clearly shows how UP is eating into India's resources rather than contributing to it.

In primary education, the condition was even worse. As per ASER survey by Pratham, not even 50 per cent of the fifth grade kids in UP could read a second grade Hindi text. In higher education 50 per cent of engineering seats in UP still go empty, as there is no proper placements, research or entrepreneurship initiatives by UP Technical University (UPTU). The only initiative taken by the Akhilesh Government is to change UPTU's name, to AKTU (Dr. A.P.J. Abdul Kalam Technical University) just to capture the legacy of Kalam sahab. In times, when states are showcasing their human resources and wooing investors and industries, Mulayam Singh Yadav, strong opponent of Rajnath Singh's anti-cheating law, seems to be content with having mafia hanging outside the windows of examination halls in Uttar Pradesh to facilitate mass cheating.

The condition of electricity in UP was also pathetic. UP needed around 25,000 MW of power and it just produces 2500 MW of electricity. It buys the rest of its electricity from outside, but still has a shortage of 5-9K MW every year. The irony is that the state was never bothered about procuring or producing the deficient amount of power, but was only focused on preparing the roaster of power distribution and power cuts. Moreover, these power cuts were decided by the regions of voters' loyalty towards the ruling parties in their respective governments.

The health infrastructure of the state was marred by NRHM scam from Mayawati era, where CMOs were being killed and still the guilty were not booked. Police recruitment Scam, Janani Suraksha Yojna Scam, Kumbh Scam and Mayawati's statue scam were the only stories the state can boast of. In fact in the Janani Suraksha Yojna scam, during Mayawati's rule, CAG report observed that to siphon money meant for pregnant and lactating women, officials had shown fake bills to claim money. Bills of District Magistrate's official car were attached as private taxi and there were cases where one woman was shown pregnant three times in one year.

The law & order situation of the state was crying for a major overhaul. National Crime Record Bureau (NCRB) data shows that Uttar Pradesh stood number one in almost all kinds of crime and that too, when there is huge under-reporting of the crime by the police officials due to political pressure during previous governments. Incidents of brutal assaults on women in Badaun, Bareilly, Bulandshahar and rioting in Muzaffarnagar and Saharanpur speaks about the total lack of spine and intent of the earlier Samajvadi Party government to govern the state.

Yadav Singh Scam, is the one that looked like it had strings connected to both the SP and the BSP party. Yadav Singh scam also speaks about the planned stoppage of the right of the people to elect members for the municipal corporation in Noida, so that the Chief Ministers of the state could directly manage the land dealings of Noida, through bureaucrats like Dr. Ramaraman, who was considered the blue eyed bureaucrat of both Mayawati and the Yadav family. This is the same Dr. Ramaraman, who was shunted and waitlisted in the very first transfer and posting government order of the Yogi government.

Akhilesh Yadav claimed in the rallies, that his government has distributed 15-18 lakh computers to the students of Uttar Pradesh. But my investigation, from my previous book, showed a very different picture. First the laptops were distributed based on the biases of voter loyalty. The RTI response received from UP government showed that the laptops that started from Lucknow for distribution, did not reach the students. Every district has a gap of 5000 to 50,000 numbers between the laptop received in the district and laptops distributed to the students. Like in Allahabad 69,395 laptops were delivered, but only 20,341 laptops were distributed, in Amethi 13,165 laptops were delivered and only 3,820 laptops were distributed, in Azamgarh 43,011 laptops were delivered and only 10,099 laptops were distributed. When I enquired further with the officials, I got a callous reply that they forgot to update the data in the system. In the field we found that, these laptops were being sold for seven to eight thousand rupees in every district of Uttar Pradesh. These laptops with stickers of Mulayam-Akhilesh duo and similar wallpaper inside seem more like a party's public relations exercise than anything else.

The 300km Agra-Lucknow expressway is always talked about as the star project of the Akhilesh government. However until the election time, this expressway was not even commissioned in its entirety. One has to switch to side lanes and under construction portions several times, while driving on it. In fact Allahabad High Court has rebuked the Samajvadi Party for falsely showcasing Agra-Lucknow expressway and Lucknow metro projects as completed projects in their electoral speeches, banners and pamphlets. Moreover when we compare this with the daily rate of construction of 20kms of national highway by Nitin Gadkari's national road department, they are making 300km of high quality national highways almost every 15 days. In the last 15 years people's expectation for development in the state of Uttar Pradesh, marred by the regional politics of caste, religion and nepotism, has dipped so low that the governments have conveniently escaped by showcasing their sub-ordinary work as their flagship projects.

In the 80's Ashish Bose had coined the term BiMaRU, for the four states of Bihar, Madhya Pradesh, Rajasthan and Uttar Pradesh, owing to their abysmal socio-economic indicators.

Since then Rajasthan and Madhya Pradesh have catapulted themselves out of the status of being diseased or BiMaRU. Bihar seemed right on track once, to come out of it, but now looks trapped again in the *chakravyuh* of kidnapping, nepotism and failed law and order with the re-entry of Lalu Prasad Yadav in Bihar politics. The state of Uttar Pradesh was, however, still screaming for development and the SP & BSP have failed miserably to live up to the mandate of the people of Uttar Pradesh for the last 15 years.

Even without access to all these macro data and facts, the people of Uttar Pradesh daily lived and observed the pathetic condition of their state. They heard '*Kam Bolta Hai*' rhetoric in Akhilesh Yadav's rallies, but while going back home from the rally, they faced bad roads, bad traffic, lawlessness, lack of electricity in their houses, corruption in the process for government jobs selection and no future for their children. It is evident that when the people of Uttar Pradesh voted for BJP, they have voted for aspirations, for a better future for their children and for a prosperous Uttar Pradesh. New Chief Minister Yogi Adityanath has huge expectations to fulfill.

Yogi's first speech after becoming Chief Minister

All these years the media has been largely focused on Yogi's fiery electoral speeches, but on 19 March, 2017, journalists were eagerly waiting for the press conference of their young saffron clad Chief Minster and listen to his government's priorities for the state.

With a pleasant and firm gesture, addressing the media persons, Yogi said[3], ".... I welcome all the friends of media in our very first press conference, along with my colleagues, Keshav Prasad Maurya ji and Dinesh Sharma ji. It's a historical day for the state of Uttar Pradesh. Bhartiya Janta Party (BJP) got unprecedented mandate in the assembly elections of 2017. The formal oath taking ceremony of the

3 Yogi Adityanath's First Press Conference As The New CM Of UP https://www.youtube.com/watch?v=9y2AEqhx53k

new government is just completed. We express our gratitude to the people of Uttar Pradesh, for giving Bhartiya Janta Party such a huge mandate, on the themes of development and good-governance. Uttar Pradesh is the birthplace and work place of Pandit Deen Dayal Upadhaya, the originator of Integral Humanism (*Ekatm Manavvad*). My government is determined to follow the path of '*Antodaya*' (upliftment of the most downtrodden), suggested by Pandit Deen Dayal Upadhaya. On this occasion we want to tell the people of the state, through you all, that my government will not leave any stone unturned for the development and prosperity of the state. My government is determined to fulfill all the promises made in our manifesto, *Lok Kalyan Sankalp Patra* of 2017. Under the able guidance of our respected Prime Minister Narendra Modi, the central government has taken a step of '*Sabka Saath Sabka Vikas*' *(Government is with everyone, Government works for everyone's development),* igniting the light of development and good-governance. State government will also serve the people of the state with the same set of ethos. You all know that in the past 15 years, Uttar Pradesh has fallen behind by miles in the race for development.

During these past years, the ruling governments have caused major distress to the people of the state by inflicting corruption, nepotism, and bad law and order situations on them. Our government will start working for the welfare of the people without any delay. My government is dedicated for the welfare of the people and will work for all sections of the society, without any discrimination. And for this we will make the government and the administration answerable and accountable to the people.

Government will work tirelessly for the basic needs of the people like food, house, roads and toilets, and will make extra effort to strengthen the law and order situation of the state. Bhartiya Janta Party government will try its best in providing the highest quality of education in the state, employment for the youth, and good quality of health and transport services for the common man on the street. Special steps will be taken for the betterment of poor, downtrodden and the backward classes. A sizable portion of state's population lives in rural areas and they are dependent on agriculture for their living. Considering this state government will make sure that agriculture will become the key to state's development. Government will take every possible step for the development of agriculture, farmers, and farm laborers. State Government will put in every possible effort for women empowerment, their security and to give them equal rights. Youth of the state had to face the ill-effects of the bad governance of the previous governments. State government will work proactively to enhance opportunities of employment for the youth of the state by providing better education and by providing skill development opportunities. The process of appointments to the government jobs will be made corruption free and transparent. We will do sustainable industrial development of the state and will create environment to attract investment in the state. And because of this, on one hand state will observe economic growth and on the other hand our youth will get the employment within the state.

And in the end I would again like to reiterate the fact that BJP respects this huge mandate given by people of Uttar Pradesh and we will not let you down. Very soon you all would see the positive effects of the new government. Today all of you have witnessed the oath ceremony of the new government. We have always talked about '*Sabka Saath Sabka Vikas' (Government is with everyone, Government works for everyone's development)*, and in the oath ceremony and in the selection of my team of ministers; you must have observed the same. Let's all work together for the betterment of our state. "Thanks to all of you...."

On being asked about his plans for the development of eastern regions of Uttar Pradesh, for primary education and health etc. Yogi replied that Bhartiya Janta Party has put its public welfare manifesto (*Lok Kalyan Sankalp Patra*) in front of the people before the elections, and whatever was promised to the people of the state will be converted into reality. He further added that, in future his senior colleagues, Mr. Siddhartha Nath Singh and Mr. Shrikant Sharma will officially brief and update the press about the cabinet meetings, decisions and various other development plans of the state government. On further questions by media, Yogi said with a confidant smile on this face that, 'For today this is enough, have faith in me and we will talk again'.

The media was pleasantly surprised to see a very different Yogi Adityanath. Yogi sounded like a perfect champion of Bhartiya Janta Party, talking of party manifesto, Pandit Deen Dayal's legacy and Prime Minister Narendra Modi's vision. He was calm, composed and talked about hard-core development challenges. During the corridor conversation after the press conference, some said that the party has tamed Yogi in bargain for the Chief Minister's position, some also said that the hardliner Yogi, is now trying to become the next development champion like Modi, some said Yogi's parliamentary interventions in last two decades as a member of parliament were unnoticed and he was always development focused, barring a few electoral speeches.

Yogi gave first interview to RSS's magazine *Panchjanya* after becoming CM

To everyone's surprise, Yogi gave his first formal print interview to RSS's flagship Hindi magazine *Panchjanya,* published on 3 April, 2017 titled – "*Homework ho chukka hai, ab bas nirnay*" (Home work is over, now is the time for decisions). Editor Hitesh Shankar and reporter Ashwini Mishra lead the interview discussion with Yogi Adityanath[4].

This was just two weeks after the government formation, but Yogi sounded quite thorough with the problems of the state and their possible set of solutions. Yogi first congratulated the *Panchjanya* family, for their bold reports on the true situation at ground zero of Uttar Pradesh during elections. Yogi then gave full credit to Amit Shah's organizational skills

4 *Home work ho chukka hai, ab bas nirnay,* http://panchjanya.com/Encyc/2017/4/3/Spi-Interview.aspx?PageType=N

and Prime Minister Narendra Modi's leadership for the Uttar Pradesh victory.

On being asked about the negative reporting, on being under constant national and international media scanner every minute after his escalation to the Chief Minister's post in the state, Yogi replied that those who are jealous of India, who can't digest development and prosperity of India, will obviously be negative on everything that is good for the country. Some people have a bias against saffron color and they will find it tough to accept him. He said that all those who were flirting with India's national security for the politics of appeasement, in the name of secularism, are facing existential crisis now. He further added that they got a huge mandate in Uttar Pradesh and they will reach the last person on the street, through various welfare and visionary schemes launched by Prime Minister Modi.

On being asked about the water scarcity and problem of mass migration in Bundelkhand region, Yogi said, "Bundelkhand and Poorvanchal regions need extra support. We have created Bundelkhand development board and Poorvanchan development board to address the challenges of these two regions. One team has already visited the region and another expert team will go soon. We are determined to solve the Bundelkhand conundrum. I myself will start my field inspections visits from Bundelkhand. For eastern Uttar Pradesh, we are strategizing to solve the issues of floods, diseases like encephalitis and problems of closing sugar mills."

On the issue of industrial growth Yogi said, "We are drafting a new industrial policy, aimed to check migration from UP. We will provide suitable platform for investors to invest in UP. We will provide security. We are going to start 'single window system' for clearance of industrial projects in the state. We will put only one condition, of giving 90 percent jobs to locals. We are happy, that we are already started getting calls from the investors. We will have two-pronged strategy. On the one hand we will attract new investment, to have new industry at new places and on the other hand we will work to strengthen traditional industry, like brass industry of Moradabad, lock industry of Aligarh, bangles industry of Firozabad and carpet industry of Bhadohi".

On the topic of sugar mills, Yogi said that they are going to inaugurate five to six new mills in next six months. This is the season for sugarcane farmers and they wanted to ensure the farmers get their dues paid on time.

On being asked about lack of opposition, as legislators from BJP and allies dominate the assembly, Yogi said, "We see assembly as a platform, where legislators from whole of the state come together, discuss issues and find solutions. We have designed a two-day training program for all the members of legislative assembly (MLAs) to enhance their knowledge on legislative work and procedures".

When asked about his views on previous government's special preference for a community for government jobs and scholarships, Yogi said that he is aware of this phenomenon. Even during the model code of conduct, by election commission of India, previous government kept their recruitment process, to favor people of a particular community for vote bank politics. He further added that they are scrutinizing the whole recruitment process. BJP government will end interviews for group 3 and group 4 jobs, to remove government discretion and to make the process transparent.

When asked about the last government's distribution of laptops, but not the electricity to charge them, Yogi said, "In our very first cabinet meeting we have decided to give 24 hours power at district headquarters, 20 hours at *tehsil* headquarters and 18 hours in villages. By 2019, we will be able to provide 24 hours electricity to whole of the state. Transformers will be repaired within 48 hours at district headquarters and with in 72 hours at rural areas. Homework is already been done on most of these things, we just need to finalize, take final decisions and move forward".

On the issue of Ram Mandir, Yogi said that he welcomes the observation of the Honorable Supreme Court to fasten the matter. As government is not party to the case, both the involved parties should resolve it through mutual discussions. If any support is required from the government, his government is ready. He added that the Honorable High Court has already given clear verdict on the dispute. Now both parties should settle it out amicably.

Yogi also talked about his government's plans for farmers, about engaging NRIs for the development of the state, defended his government's move to stop illegal slaughterhouses on environmental grounds, ruled out any possibility of success for any opportunistic *maha gathbandhan (mega coalition)* by opposition parties in future elections.

While finishing the interview when *Panchjanya* team asked, "What is the 'Yogi-mantra' for governance?" To this, he said that they have to bring back good-governance in the state. Corruption free system and crime free society is their first priority and they are getting very suitable guidance from PM Modi led central government for the same.

This first print interview with *panchjanya*, after becoming the Chief Minister, gave an insight into Yogi's priorities. This interview became important, as it was the first opportunity for the people to know, Yogi, the Chief Minister, who is talking the right language of governance now.

Yogi's Initial Days as Chief Minister of Uttar Pradesh

Yogi Adityanath has lived a life of a yogi, since his arrival to the Gorakhdham mutt in 1994. He works for 18-20 hours a day and expects the same from his team. In a departmental meeting, Adityanath said those officers who cannot work 18-20 hours a day are free to leave. The state government staff began sticking to 9am to 6pm duty hours in offices, following surprise inspections by various Ministers. From day one, Yogi and his ministers have been on the job, conducting field inspections, office inspection, sending notices, making presentations and meeting people. I will now take my readers through the early days of Yogi *sarkar*.

Late night departmental presentations

It is still early to give any verdict on the Yogi government, but the initial months of Yogi *sarkar* look very promising. Even the detractors are pleasantly surprised by his administrative skills, focused moves and diligence in governance. In the first month, all the ministers of Yogi Government spent time in learning about each other's department in detail like studious students with Chief Minister himself present during all the departmental presentations. Deputy Chief Minister, Dinesh Sharma said in an interview to a TV channel, "The starting time of these presentation sessions was fixed at 6pm, but end time was not fixed. Sometimes they ended at 11pm in the night and sometime they went beyond to the next day". Senior officials of the state and senior officers at the Chief Minister's office attended these presentations and each minister and his team made their best attempt to present the achievements, challenges and 100 days' plan of their department. One officer revealed anonymously that at these presentation the Ministers intervened, asked counter questions, debated, argued, pointed out field realities and gave suggestions as well. These rigorous presentations sessions proved to be very productive for all the ministers to get to know each other, to know each other's strength, to know each other's departments and most importantly to know the priorities of their boss – Yogi Adityanath. During this presentation to everybody's surprise Yogi displayed amazing administrative knowledge, deep understanding of budgetary processes and of government procedures. Yogi's team mates and the bureaucracy have realized that his two decades of tireless interventions in the parliament, his ground work in his constituency and administration of various large scale institutions of the ancient Gorakhnath Mutt, made him a natural leader and an able administrator.

Mr. S.P. Singh Baghel[5], one of the senior ministers in Yogi Cabinet, who has spent years in the Samajvadi Party and Bahujan Samaj Party, when asked during the

---

5 Panchayat AajTak, 5th May, 2017 – https://www.youtube.com/watch?v=Jlbp-BR1VL8

AajTak *Panchayat*, interview about the differences he see in the governance style, replied that during, Mayawati's government, cabinet used to sit for 3.5 to 7 minutes, during Mulayam's time, cabinet used to sit for 15 minutes and now let alone the cabinet meeting, even for departmental presentations, all the Ministers and senior officers are sitting till late night. On a lighter note, Mr Baghel added that a very few of them may have seen back-to-back shows at 6pm and 9pm of even the super hit movies, but they all sat from 6pm to 12am for a month to understand each other's department and to learn about the government. Mr Baghel further added, that during Mayawati's days there was no opportunity even for the party MLAs to meet the Chief Minister. Mayawati could only summon them, causing palpitations to the legislators of any unexpected outcome. In contrast now Chief Minister Yogi has designated special days and time slots to meet MLAs and MPs of the state.

Janta Darbars

Listening to people's problems and resolving them is not new to Yogi Adityanath. He has carried his habit from two long decades as a parliamentarian in his constituency, of organizing a regular Janta Darbar[6]. Recently in an interview with Rajat Sharma[7], Yogi told that these Janta Darbars always helped him to keep a tab on the pulse of the people and know the performance of public offices and officers. Yogi further narrated that recently a cancer patient came to the Janta Darbar in Lucknow, to seek help for the deadly disease. Yogi thought he could refer the patient to the new cancer hospital inaugurated by the previous Akhilesh government. Yogi asked the concerned minister to visit the hospital and see the arrangements. Yogi said he was shocked, when his minister reported him back, that only the hospital building was erected. There is no chemotherapy equipment, no

6 Yogi's Janta Darbar. http://indiatoday.intoday.in/video/lucknow-yogi-adityanath-janta-darbar-uttar-pradesh/1/919196.html

7 UP Chief Minister Yogi Adityanath in Aap Ki Adalat, India TV https://www.youtube.com/watch?v=xshgEQfGca4&t=3s

radiology, no doctors and no staff. Some beds were brought from KGMU hospital for the inauguration day and were returned later.

During the same interview Yogi said, he daily meets 25-30 Muslim women in his Janta Darbar, who come with their fathers, mothers, brothers or relatives. All of them have the same problem. They all narrate that how their husbands have given them *talaq* (divorce) on phone or on a piece of paper.

Following the Chief Minister, the ministers in his government are also meeting commoners in their work offices and they are also sitting in BJP's state office, on a rotation basis to listen to the problems of the common man.

Yogi and Uttar Pradesh's Bureaucracy

The new Chief Ministers usually begin their stint by overhauling the bureaucracy, but Adityanath did not make changes immediately after assuming office. He retained the former Chief Minister Akhilesh Yadav's set-up, but warned officers against laxity. However in the second week of April, three weeks after taking charge, Yogi moved 20 senior IAS officers, putting 8 of them on the wait-list. Among the wait-listed officers the names that cannot be missed are Dr. Ramaraman of Noida Authority fame and Navneet Sehgal, who were favored by the previous dispensation. These are the same two names, which Amar Singh had loudly proclaimed as the most corrupt bureaucrats of Uttar Pradesh in the famous 'Aap Ki Adalat'[8] episode with Rajat Sharma. Though many BJP loyalists believe that only wait listing them is not a solution, but such officers should be prosecuted for their blatant corruption and misuse of power.

To tighten the law and order situation of Uttar Pradesh, Yogi brought, one of the senior most IPS officer, Sulkhan Singh, from the 1980 batch to replace the much junior Director General Of Police (DGP) of Uttar Pradesh, Javed Ahmed from the 1984 batch. During the recent assembly polls, the BJP had petitioned the Election Commission to

8 Amar Singh in Aap Ki Adalat 2017 (Full Episode) https://www.youtube.com/watch?v=C5U4JrKjCyw

remove Ahmed, alleging that he was working at the behest of the then Samajvadi Party government. On the contrary, Sulkhan Singh is known for his honesty and dedication. His paternal house in Banda, is still made of *kaprail,* the old style tiles made in the rural parts. His only big asset is a house that he purchased from Lucknow Development Authority (LDA) for which he is still paying the EMIs. Sulkhan Singh is known in the state as someone who does not succumb to political pressure and follow the rules book to the T. Sulkhan Singh's honesty has remained a hindrance to his career so far. If Sulkhan Singh had not exposed the police recruitment scam under Mulayam governance in 2007, he would have become the DGP much earlier[9]. By bringing him at the helm of affairs of Uttar Pradesh police department, Yogi has made his intentions clear.

Shashi Prakash Goyal, an IAS topper of 1989-batch, officer of UP cadre who has returned from a central posting recently, has been made the new principal secretary to the CM. Goyal will also be the Principal Secretary to departments of Civil Aviation, Estate and Protocol.

Yogi Adityanath has also brought 1987 batch, senior IAS officer Avneesh Awashthi, to head the very important -Information Division for the government. Mr Awashthi is an IITian and previously held the charge of District Magistrate of Gorakhpur.

Young and bright 1995 batch IAS officer, Mrityunjay Kumar was appointed the Secretary to the Chief Minister. Mrityunjay has a Bachelor in Engineering and Masters in Public Policy and Administration from Kings College, London. Mrityunjay is very tech-savvy and won highest category platinum award for his innovative e-governance initiatives under 'Digital India Awards', 2016.

Amit Singh of Indian Railway Services, who was serving as Regional Passport Officer in Lucknow was also pulled into Chief Minister's office. Senior IAS officer Nitish Kumar has been appointed as a Special Secretary to the Chief Minister.

9 http://www.indiasamvad.co.in/special-stories/sulkhan-singh-appointed-as-up-police-dgp-yogi-govt-21362

Prior to this, Kumar was posted as the Additional Registrar of Cooperative Societies.

The very first appointment in the Chief Minister Secretariat was Rigzin Samphel, as the Special Secretary to the Uttar Pradesh Chief Minister Yogi Adityanath. A 2003-batch IAS officer, Samphel was also among the top officials during Samajwadi Party government and has served as the District Magistrate of Jalaun district in Bundelkhand region of Uttar Pradesh in the year 2002.

Rajbhushan Singh Rawat, a close associate of Yogi Adityanath and also his classmate from college days, has also moved to Lucknow to assist Yogi in his work.

Office space, Punctuality and Financial Hygiene

Pankaj Jaiswal of Hindustan Times wrote[10] that in just a month in office, Adityanath has set a scorching pace for his initiatives, from banning *paan* and *gutkha* at government offices to ensuring strict working hours are adhered by latecomers. Various decisions were taken in the initial days of Yogi assuming office. An hour after he took oath on March 19, Adityanath ordered all Ministers to declare their income, movable and immovable properties within 15 days. He has asked them to submit the declarations to the CM Secretariat. He made it clear that his government will have zero tolerance to corruption. Adityanath administered an oath of cleanliness and honesty to his Ministers. He has fixed Friday as the day when the state staff must tidy up their workspaces. He has asked them to devote two hours per week to cleanliness. He has also asked them to read the BJP's 2017 poll manifesto and mull over how to implement them in their respective departments, besides making budgetary provisions for it.

In a recent interview with India TV[11] Yogi told that in the previous government Ministers, including the Chief Minister

---

10 Top 16 decisions in 30 days: Yogi Adityanath's first month as Uttar Pradesh CM http://www.hindustantimes.com/lucknow/16-decisions-in-30-days-yogi-adityanath-s-first-month-as-uttar-pradesh-chief-minister/story-ie7VVu00sxZJB7KjLj2g2N.html

11 https://www.youtube.com/watch?v=xshgEQfGca4&t=3s

rarely came to office. They all operated from their camp (home) offices at their leisure. To emphasize his point Yogi narrated an incident, that during the previous government's rule, when he met the then agriculture minister, agriculture secretary and agriculture commissioner at Gorakhpur railway station he was surprised to discover that in spite of being in his role for six months, minister's officials did not know him by face. Yogi had to introduce them to each other. Yogi said that now this all has changed and that they have stopped the camp office culture in the whole state.

The Yogi government has also made a citizen charter for the quick movements of files. According to the charter a file should not spend more than three days on any desk. Even the department head should clear it maximum within seven days.

On March 21, Adityanath went to Delhi to meet Prime Minister Narendra Modi to discuss distribution of portfolios to his Ministers. He also informed the PM that MPs were lobbying for transfers, postings of officers. Modi, on March 23, ordered all MPs not to interfere in transfers and postings.

While the opposition parties are busy criticizing Yogi to keep themselves relevant, Yogi remains unfazed by all the criticism and his government is moving on with unprecedented pace of governance. Decisions to fulfill the poll promises are being taken and a focused 100 days plan is being designed for the different ministries.

Crackdown on Illegal Slaughterhouses

Banning illegal slaughterhouses was the most talked about thing of BJP's 2017-election manifesto. CM Yogi Adityanath ordered a crackdown on illegal slaughterhouses, meat shops and cow smuggling in the very first month of assuming office. This decision has faced quite a lot of backlash. The government has clarified that only illegal slaughterhouses were targeted. The protection of cows and calves is also one of the directive principles of state policy contained in Article 48 of the Constitution. However, a blanket ban remains very much a state subject. Various states have chosen to outlaw cow slaughter, as per local customs and culinary preferences. Many people may not know that cow slaughter is illegal in Uttar Pradesh, as it is in most parts of India, since 1955. Uttar Pradesh Prevention of Cow Slaughter Act, 1955[12] governs the rules around slaughter of cattle in the state. As per this act, slaughtering cows (including a heifer and calf) is prohibited. Transport of cow outside the state for slaughter is also not permitted.

As Firstpost staff reported[13], it is important to point out, at the onset, that the issue of slaughterhouses is also about the environmental norms, blatantly flouted by the illegal units, usually in connivance with local administration and politicians. Even though much of the debate has bordered around the religious sentiments of the Hindu community, which revers the cow, a much-neglected aspect is its environmental implications. Slaughterhouses are listed under the 'red' category (amid those industries with highest release of effluents and pollutants in environment) of industries, which are considered heavily polluting and are covered under the central action plan for consent management. This essentially means that slaughterhouses are counted amid industries that are most polluting for water bodies, and if unregulated can be a serious menace to public health. According to a list put out by the Uttar Pradesh Pollution Control Board (UPPCB) in 2015, of the 129 industrial units (deemed very hazardous for the environment) that have not installed anti-pollution devices, 44 units were slaughterhouses.

While researching for the book, I visited the Gorakhdham mutt in Gorakhpur, and found that spending time with cows in the Mutt's *gau-shala* (cow shelter) was an integral part of Yogi Adityanath's daily routine. So his personal indulgence in banning illegal cow slaughterhouses looks natural. I will not be surprised, if in future we see stricter implementation of

12 http://nyaaya.in/law/979/the-uttar-pradesh-prevention-of-cow-slaughter-act-1955/#section-2

13 http://www.firstpost.com/india/up-slaughterhouse-crackdown-here-is-all-you-need-to-know-about-the-laws-regulating-abattoirs-3356182.html

Uttar Pradesh Prevention of Cow Slaughter Act, 1955, under Yogi Adityanath's leadership.

Truth Behind Illegal Slaughterhouses

To open a slaughterhouse in India, the applicant is required to apply for land use clearance for opening the unit. However, it is after this step that a series of checks and norms kick in that are specific to this industry. According to Uttar Pradesh's Department of Infrastructure and Industrial development, a No Objection Certificate (NOC) must be obtained from the district authorities and the UPPCB, both of which carry out separate inspections to determine whether the unit is being built in accordance with the set norms.

After UPPCB grants an environmental clearance, the plant owner is then required to approach the Agricultural and Processed Food Products Export Development Authority (APEDA), the Union government's body that regulates the export of all products. Before granting approval for export of the meat, APEDA has its own procedures and series of checks and inspections, which are carried out before an NOC is granted.

The slaughterhouses should further operate in accordance with the Prevention of Cruelty to Animals (Slaughter House) Rules, 2001, that outlines further laws to ensure the health and well being of cattle being slaughtered. Amid other things, it requires a large and airy reception, and resting area for the cattle and a compulsory examination by a veterinary doctor, 24 hours before they are slaughtered.

Moreover, a slaughterhouse should also be licensed and registered with the Food Safety and Standards Authority of India (FSSAI), under the

Food Safety (License and Registration of Food Business) Regulations Act, 2011.

Besides, even after the slaughterhouses have obtained all these clearances, they are required to maintain standards of operations in accordance with the environmental, hygiene and sanitation, and prevention of animal cruelty norms in their day to day operation.

In May 2015, hearing a plea of an environmental activist, the National Green Tribunal (NGT) had ruled that any slaughterhouse that is operating without the necessary permission from local authorities — particularly the UPPCB — should not be allowed to operate. According to a report in The Indian Express, it is this order that the UP government has cited time and again in justifying its action against the slaughterhouses. The NGT also asked UPPCB to form a committee that will issue certificates to small shops on a quarterly basis.

The NGT order came because of a petition that alleged that "the abattoirs were discharging untreated effluents contaminated with animal waste and blood of slaughtered animals in open drains which go into the tributaries of Ganga and Yamuna, polluting them," according to a PTI report at the time published in OneIndia.

"As per official records, more than 8.5 lakhs cattle are slaughtered annually in Uttar Pradesh, at its 115 registered slaughterhouses. However, a bare perusal of the records of total export made by the state shows that it is several times higher than the amount mentioned in the records and data maintained by UP," the petitioner had said.

There are no records of illegal slaughterhouses available officially. However, according to industry insiders, there could be an estimated 140 slaughterhouses and over 50,000 meat shops that don't have permission to operate. In the current crackdown, the government has rounded up more than 20 illegal slaughterhouses and several meat shops.

Oblivious of all the facts, popular media and opposition parties are busy coloring Yogi Adityanath as anti-minority.

Anti-Romeo squads

BJP's *Lok Kalyan Sankalp Patra* also talked about establishing 'anti-Romeo squads' in the state, keeping women's safety in mind. The National Commission for Women (NCW) has claimed that Uttar Pradesh has the highest number of criminal cases against women. Rekha Sharma[14], a member of the NCW, said at a press conference that on an average 60 per cent of the complaints received by the NCW are from UP. She said Ghaziabad tops the list among the cities in UP, with at least 50 complaints every month. As per National Crime Records Bureau (NCRB) data, UP tops the chart for crime committed against women. NCRB stated that UP had filed 35,527 cases of crime committed against women in the year 2015 that contributed to 10.9 per cent of all cases in India, higher than any other state. In his very first week, the CM asked to set up 'anti-Romeo squads' across the state for the protection of women against harassment.

Anti-Romeo squads' actions created some confusion due to the way the police responded in some cases. In response to that Adityanath on March 25 ordered the framing of guidelines and asked the police to be rational while implementing it. The composition of the 'anti-Romeo squads' is a team of 2 police people, mostly a male and a female. Two to three teams are to be deployed in the jurisdiction of one police station. Number of teams deployed would depend on

14 Crime against women highest in Uttar Pradesh: NCWhttp://indiatoday.intoday.in/story/crime-against-women-highest-in-uttar-pradesh-ncw/1/733934.html

the number of schools and colleges in the area. Squads will move around near schools and colleges where there are larger numbers of women. Their task is to identify eve teasers and troublemakers in a crowd. They will move around in uniform and in some cases in plain clothes. Teams will comprise of constables, head constables, ASI and SI. Anti-Romeo squads can let off miscreants with a warning, can inform parents and even initiate criminal action depending on the seriousness of the case.

Tightening Law & Order in the state

Yogi government has shown utmost focus on tightening the law and order structure in the state. Brining Sulkhan Singh at the helm of affairs showed Yogi's tough intentions for the task. District Magistrates (DMs) and Superintendents of Police (SPs) are advised to meet people daily form 9 AM to 11AM and stop the camp office culture. In a recent interview to India TV, Yogi said that it is shameful for any government if it can't provide protection to its citizens. When asked about the recent incidents of various criminal cases, Yogi said that this is the last set of attempts by the criminals, as they are being pushed against the wall by the police force. Yogi emphasized that now criminals are facing the bullets of the police force instead of political protection.

Unlike in previous governments, we are observing the closure the cases at a faster pace. Criminals of Mathura jewelers' murder case were traced within 5 days. A trader kidnaped from Firozabad was rescued within hours. An Innova car looted near Etawa, on Lucknow-Agra expressway was recovered and perpetrators arrested with in four hours. Police looks active and vigilant under Yogi and his DGP Sulkhan Singh.

Pothole free roads

Pothole free road connectivity is a boon for farmers to get their produce to *mandis* on time; it's a boon for students to reach colleges, patients to reach hospitals, office commuters to get to work on time. And no one understands this better than

CM Yogi Adityanath, who has spent the last two decades on road, listening to and addressing people's problems. 'Pothole free roads' is one of the major challenges Yogi gave to his Public Works Department (PWD) Minister and his deputy, Keshav Prasad Maurya. On March 25, Adityanath set a deadline, of June 15, 2017, to make all the roads of UP, pothole-free. In fact while talking to Rahul Kanwal on AajTak Panchayat[15], Yogi Adityanath asked him to send their teams on roads, film the potholes and send that information to his office, so that no pothole is missed.

Farmer's Loan Waiver

During campaigning for 2017 assembly elections, eastern UP was very crucial for BJP. The districts going to polls in the sixth phase were Mau, Maharajganj, Kushinagar, Gorakhpur, Deoria, Azamgarh and Ballia. Azamgarh alone has 10 Assembly seats, of which Samajvadi Party had won nine in 2012. But this time Mulayam Singh Yadav did not address a single meeting in his parliamentary constituency. While campaigning for these 49 Assembly seats for the 6th phase of Uttar Pradesh elections, Prime Minister Narendra Modi addressed a public rally in Deoria in Uttar Pradesh on 1st March. The Prime Minister understood that this crucial region is heavily populated by farmers. He boldly declared that, if BJP comes to power, they will waive farmers' loan in the first cabinet meeting after the results of UP and will clear all *bakaya* (due) amount of sugarcane farmers within 120 days. These were two important promises for the large farming community of Uttar Pradesh and true to their word, the Uttar Pradesh government decided to waive farm loans totaling Rs 36,359 crores, in its very first cabinet meeting on 4 April. The decision is expected to benefit at least 2.2 crore small and marginal farmers of the state. Other state governments could now come under pressure for a similar waiver. In Maharashtra, ruled by a BJP-Shiv Sena coalition, Sena Chief Uddhav Thackeray was quick to congratulate Adityanath for implementing the

15 Exclusive: Yogi Adityanath Speaks At 'Panchayat AajTak' – Uttar Pradesh https://www.youtube.com/watch?v=YFf2rbQy2UI

poll promise. He asked Maharashtra Chief Minister Devendra Fadnavis to also waive farm loans, reported Gyan Varma and Anuja of The Live Mint[16].

Apart from loan relief, the government announced setting up of 5,000 wheat procurement centres across the state and projected that it will buy 80 lakh metric tonnes from farmers. It was also announced that the government will buy potato at Rs 487 per quintal from farmers.

The decision of farm loan waiver faced mixed response. The so-called left intellectuals of Jawaharlal Nehru University (JNU), who were unable to digest a saffron clad Chief Minister and who have supported and vouched for similar waivers and subsidies in past, are now singing a different tune. Himanshu, an associate professor at Jawaharlal Nehru University, Delhi, told the Mint reporter that farmers need to be supported and a loan waiver is required at this point of time, but the government needs to look at a long-term solution for the problem of low farming incomes. The basic question is, why are farmers getting into a debt trap so soon, and unless the government looks at that, there will be no substantial relief. Frequent loan waivers create a problem of moral hazard and similar demands are likely to come from states like Maharashtra, Tamil Nadu, Karnataka and Andhra Pradesh where farmers are affected.

On the other hand, Congress Chief Spokesperson Randeep Surjewala said in a statement: "UP government's first cabinet meeting has shattered the hopes of the farmers. Yogi-led cabinet has decided to waive off loans of just Rs 36,000 crore which will neither free the farmers of their loans nor will it give them enough relief".

Payment to Sugarcane Farmers

Similar speed was shown in the other poll promise made by PM Modi for the Sugar cane farmers. Mills were been given a stipulated time to clear the arrears and what followed

16 Yogi Adityanath govt decides to waive farm loans in Uttar Pradesh: http://www.livemint.com/Politics/orUS3U8zWFgsaGkuNrxP7N/Yogi-Adityanath-cabinet-waives-off-farm-loans-up-to-Rs-1-lak.html

is history. More than Rs 5,000 crore was paid by the mill owners in a matter of a few weeks. Sugarcane Development Minister, Suresh Rana proudly tweeted[17]- "Rs 5080 crore debt is being paid by 56 Sugar Mills to Cane farmers!". And the mill owners, who did not comply with the deadline, faced the consequences. An FIR was lodged against a Bajaj Hindusthan-owned sugar mill in Muzaffarnagar district. The case was lodged under the Essential Commodities Act, among others, for allegedly diverting funds meant for settling farmers' arrears to other businesses. The case has been filed against the mill promoter and the occupiers, reported Virendra Singh Rawat[18] of Business Standard.

Power for all

Within the first month of joining office, the Adityanath government also signed an agreement with the Centre assuring 24-hour power supply to the district headquarters, 20-hour supply at *tehsil* level and in Bundelkhand region, and 18 hours in rural areas. The government declared that by November 2018, all the villages and households in the state would get 24-hour power supply. This comes as a major relief for the people of Uttar Pradesh especially during the summers. In a recent interview on India TV[19], Yogi said that the government has managed to purchase enough power to execute the declared roaster. He further said that they need to reduce line losses. Yogi told the channel that the earlier governments were in the habit of stealing, and the people did the same as well. In the Akhilesh government era there was 80-90 percent power theft in the districts like Rampur, Azamgarh, Badaun, Kannaujand Etawa. Yogi added that now this all will stop and that they will move confidently towards 'Power for All' by 2018.

---

17 https://twitter.com/SureshRanaBJP/status/855986541792944128/photo/1

18 http://www.business-standard.com/article/economy-policy/up-sugarcane-arrears-breach-rs-6-000-crore-mark-117040300706_1.html

19 https://www.youtube.com/watch?v=xshgEQfGca4&t=3s

Investigation on corruption cases

During the departmental presentations Yogi and his team also noticed various anomalies in the projects executed by the previous governments and the CM ordered probes into a couple of them. During the departmental review of the Cane Development and Sugar Industry Department, team took cognizance of the fact that 21 sugar mills were sold at a throwaway price by former Chief Minister Mayawati. This angered Yogi and during the meeting he said that nobody can be allowed to sell government properties at dirt cheap rates as the property belonged to the people. He also said that he will not hesitate in ordering a Central Bureau of Investigation (CBI) probe into the matter, in which even the Comptroller and Auditor General (CAG) have pointed out heavy irregularities. IANS[20] reported that, The Rs 1,180-crore scam has been hanging heavy on the former Chief Minister Mayawati, but it was put in cold storage by the earlier Akhilesh Yadav-led Samajwadi Party government. Despite serious lapses coming to light in the probe ordered then, the SP government chose not to act against political rival and Bahujan Samaj Party Chief Mayawati in the sale of these sugar mills. The mills belonged to the UP State Sugar Corporation Ltd and the state Sugar and Cane Development Corporation. Complaints made on the scam alleged that huge kickbacks were paid to the 'powerful' in the then BSP government to get the sale deal through. Former Chief Minister Akhilesh Yadav had handed over the probe into the alleged irregularities in the sale of sugar mills, to the Lokayukta in November 2012, but despite a yearlong drawn probe, Justice N.K. Mehrotra had not fixed responsibility for the loss to the exchequer on anyone.

Adityanath had earlier expressed dissatisfaction over the progress of the Akhilesh Yadav government's Gomti riverfront project. Ganesh Kumar[21]and Radha Udayakumar

---

20 http://www.newindianexpress.com/nation/2017/apr/08/up-cm-yogi-adityanath-orders-probe-into-mayawatis-sale-of-sugar-mills-1591414.html

21 http://indiatoday.intoday.in/story/yogi-adityanath-investigation-gomti-river-front-uttar-pradesh-bjp/1/918145.html

of India Today reported that the project was launched to channelize the river by constructing a diaphragm wall and by landscaping and constructing intercepting drains on both banks. In a recent interview with Rajat Sharma[22], Yogi told that the PPR (Pre Project Report) of this project was budgeted at rupees 150 crores, but the DPR (Detailed Project Report) reached rupees 600 crores and after two years had lapsed, and with over rupees 1,427 crores spent; only 60 per cent of the work was completed. A demand of an additional amount of rupees 1,500 crores was being made for the project, which was initially scheduled to be completed by May 2017. Moreover the aim of the project should have been cleaning the water and blocking the drains discharging sewage into the river, but that was not done. Yogi further commented that the work was being carried out without keeping the main goal of the project in mind and instead, funds were being used on unproductive things such as erecting fountains and other decorative structures.

Yogi's first big TV interview after six weeks of Yogi Sarkar

On May 6, 2017, Yogi Adityanath, was interviewed by Rahul Kanwal on Aaj Tak Panchayat[23] and summing up the initial six weeks of his government, Yogi gave a detailed account of his government's work and future plans. This was an important interview, as it was the first major TV interview of Yogi Adityanath after completing initial weeks in the office. This interview gave a sense on Yogi government's working style, pace, direction, vision and priorities. I am presenting some important excerpts from the interview, for my readers.

Rahul: There is no other Chief Minister in the whole country who has this much craze. After becoming the Chief Minister

22 https://www.youtube.com/watch?v=xshgEQfGca4

23 Exclusive: Yogi Adityanath Speaks At 'Panchayat AajTak' – Uttar Pradesh https://www.youtube.com/watch?v=YFf2rbQy2UI

this is the first time Yogi Adityanath will be answering the questions on a large public platform. There are a lot of questions. What is in Yogi's heart? How will Uttar Pradesh (UP) become *Uttam Pradesh* (Better State)? Yogi Ji you are most welcome on Aajtak, India Today's U.P *Panchayat*. Before you several Chief Ministers have come and gone and every one assured to make Uttar Pradesh an *Uttam* Pradesh. Everybody tried his or her best, but no one succeeded in making it an *Uttam* Pradesh. How much do you believe that in Yogi-raj (Yogi's rule) Uttar Pradesh will become *Uttam* Pradesh and before the end of your tenure UP can come out of the tag of being one of the diseased states (BiMaRU)[24].

Yogi Adityanath: Dear brothers and sisters, we are all present here at the *Panchayat* organized by Aajtak- India Today group. Under the guidance of our Honorable Prime Minister, Narendra Modi, 22 crore people of Uttar Pradesh have given Bhartiya Janta Party a huge mandate and after such a humongous mandate our honorable Prime Minister and the National President of BJP, Mr Amit Shah have believed in me. Now my team and I will work hard to live up to the expectations of 22 crore people of Uttar Pradesh and I believe that in the last month and a half there already has been some difference.

Every one of you has seen that whenever new Chief Ministers come, they disturb the whole system like a house of cards. But we have extracted work from the existing machinery without making any major changes in the bureaucracy. Wherever there was a burning requirement only after one month we started making changes. We have only moved those people out, who were not ready to change themselves or who were not comfortable with this new disciplined system. We are guided by Prime Minister Modi's mantra of *'Sabka Saath, Sabka Vikas'*. I believe that *Jungle Raj* of Uttar Pradesh will soon be over and we are already striding towards that goal. I am aware that a few untoward

---

24 BiMaRU stands for Bihar, Madhya Pradesh, Rajasthan and Uttar Pradesh

incidents are still happening, but I assure you that when I come in front of media after the 100 days of the government then every daughter and mother, every businessman and youth will feel safe on the streets of Uttar Pradesh.

Uttar Pradesh currently is a diseased and deficient state. Taking UP out of this condition is one of the major challenges that we are working on. I strongly believe that in a state like Uttar Pradesh strengthening law and order should be our foremost priority and we are firming up our plans for the same.

In the last 15 years, transfers and postings have become a business in Uttar Pradesh. We have come up with a new transfer policy so that no one can make money in transfers and postings. Now when an official is shifted, the concerned Minister should know the reason and it will also be reported to my office and me. The reason and benefits of every transfer will be looked into before making the decision. Hard working individuals are most welcome in my team and I will be glad to drop others to their homes.

For a state like Uttar Pradesh we need to have our priorities decided. We will work for farmers, for the youth, for the development and problems of the common man and to end the VIP culture. Security should not be anyone's status symbol and the criminals will never get any protection from the administration. Government will not protect the criminals, and no one will be allowed to take the law and order in their own hands. I am reiterating that, police under our government will not show any bias on the basis of caste, religion or gender.

In spite of immense natural resources and fertile land, farmers of Uttar Pradesh are devastated. Uttar Pradesh has been unsuccessful in properly utilizing its agriculture resources. In extreme conditions, unfortunately farmers see suicide as the only option. Many farmers have committed suicide in different parts of UP in the last five years. For the immediate relief of the farmers, we took a huge step of waiving off farmers' loan. Honorable Prime Minister Narendra Modi says that government's work should be for people's benefit and not just for publicity. To provide long-term solutions to farmers, we have taken some steps on priority, like to give them the appropriate prices for their crops. We are taking various steps to double farmers' income by 2022. In the last six weeks, we have opened more than 5000 wheat purchase centers to buy crops directly from the farmers. Until now farmers used to sell their crop through agents and never got the right price for their produce. If the actual amount payable to farmers was rupees 1400, they only got around rupees 1200 or rupees 1100. We have decided to transfer the amount directly to the farmer's banks account through RTGS. If the actual price of wheat is rupees 1625 per quintal then he should get nothing less than rupees 1625. Government will also add an extra of ten rupees per quintal for washing the wheat. Several agents have approached us, saying that till last year all the purchase was made through them. We have rejected all such offers and opened 5000 crops purchase centers where the farmers can directly sell their yield and we have been successful in doing that.

Sometimes open markets may pay more than the government. We have kept both options open for the farmers. If they are getting good price in market, they can sell in the markets, and if no one is buying their produce then government will purchase it from them. This is the first time that this movement has began on such a big scale and in comparison to last year we have purchased four times more wheat through different government recognized centers of the state.

We have made a strategy to facilitate clearance of pending payments of sugarcane farmers of the state. We have cleared more than 6000 crores of the sugarcane farmers' pending payments and some 4000 crores still remains. We are in talks with the concerned mill owners to resolve the matter through discussion and after that the government will take further stricter actions against the defaulting mills.

For the first time in the history of Uttar Pradesh the right price of potato is announced and today I am happy that the farmers are able to sell their potatoes for more than the government's price. We have also designed strategies to protect farmers from floods. Such measures were not event discussed in UP in the last 15 years.

As there is no electricity, roads are bad and law and order condition is pathetic, no one was ready to invest in Uttar Pradesh. For power, we have taken immediate steps. The state has 75 districts and the electricity will be distributed to all the districts without any bias. On the occasion of *Babasahab Bhimrao Ambedkar's Jayanti,* we have started giving 24 hours power to all the district headquarters, 20 hours to the *tehsils and in the Bundelkhand region* and in rural areas there will be 18 hours of uninterrupted electricity. To increase people's participation, we will incentivize rural areas with 24 hours power, if there is significant drop in line loss in their area.

Simultaneously some of our agencies are working tirelessly to improve the road infrastructure. We are creating a completely new environment for the investors. A group of Ministers are working on a new industrial policy. In the coming five years, these investors will generate more than 70 lacs jobs in the state.

I was amused that in the past, the Mining Minister had more property than that of the mining budget of the state, but we are stopping all this. We have managed to place e-tendering system in all ministries. All the tenders above one lakh must be executed through e-tendering. All this while, the districts where mining is possible were poor districts. We have started a 'district mineral fund' for all such mining districts to facilitate development there.

In the report published yesterday, you all must have seen that in the 100 clean cities of the country only one city from Uttar Pradesh managed to make it to the list i.e. Varanasi. However in the 100 dirtiest cities of the country there are 52 cities of Uttar Pradesh. My team has prepared a comprehensive plan on this, after a detailed discussion. We have instructed the minister in-charge of the districts to take the message of cleanliness to their respective districts to make UP a clean state. I will start this massive drive from tomorrow by cleaning four places in Lucknow myself. However, we are determined that before the 31 December 2017, we will attempt to make 30 districts of the state 'Open Defecation Free (ODF) and by 2 October, 2018 all the districts of Uttar Pradesh will be fully equipped with public toilets. I am confident that by next year there will be more than 50 cities from Uttar Pradesh listed among the 100 clean cities of the country. Our frame of mind to execute our plans is completely positive and there is no place for any negativity. I seek the support of senior citizens, experts from different sectors and specially friends from media to make Uttar Pradesh rank first in the '*Swacch Bharat Abhiyan*' of Honorable Prime Minster. We will take this movement forward with full zeal. Our team under the guidance of the central Urban Development Minister soon will visit Goa, Bengaluru and Nagpur where there is robust policy for Solid Waste Management. We are able to collect waste from a particular area, but we have no idea of what to do with that waste. The waste collected from door to door can be converted into compost and can also be used to generate electricity.

The other day, I went to examine the Gomti River Front. I was shocked to observe that, the task of cleaning of Gomti river was budgeted at Rs 600 crores and the work is still incomplete even after spending Rs 1400 crores. When I enquired from the concerned officials about drainage of sewers of Lucknow, they did not have an exact strategy. They will have to drain them into the river Gomti itself. I said that Gomti river is a tributary of river Ganga that joins Ganga in Jaunpur and all this dirty water will go into the Ganga. If that was the case, what will happen to the '*Namami Gange Pariyojna*' (Clean Ganga Project)? They had no reply to offer.

We are going to make a solid strategy for the Gomti River. We are going to setup STPs (Sewage treatment Plants) near sources of garbage. Difficult part is to manage the operating cost of these STPs. At many places STPs are installed, but they are not in working conditions. They are only for show. We have asked to make an engineering strategy, which can generate energy out of waste, to manage the operating costs of these STPs. There are 1685 villages on the banks of river Ganga, spread across 15 districts. We are determined to equip all these 1685 villages with toilets before 15 May, 2017.

Various such programs have been started and accelerated to make Uttar Pradesh a clean Uttar Pradesh and a capable Uttar

Pradesh. I am present here to seek your support and I believe that my government will get all your support. Thank you.

Rahul: Yogi Ji since you have become the Chief Minister, its being said that you wake up at 3 AM in the morning and start meetings at 7 AM. Some bureaucrats complain that you start the meetings early and the day ends only at 12 or 1 in the night. Is it just the starting spirit or do you believe that you will work at this speed for all the 5 years?

Yogi Adityanath: See, this is integral to my work ethic. My work starts early in the morning. In Gorakhpur, I had cow-sheds, agricultural fields and I would to spend my time there. But in Lucknow I don't have them. I don't have any temple here. I have the responsibility of my party to make the whole state a temple and my team and I will put in all the energy required to deliver the same.

Rahul: You said you would make the all the villages along river Ganga, Open Defecation Free before the 15 May. Similarly you said you will get the potholes on the roads of Uttar Pradesh filled before the 15 June. During the elections in Uttar Pradesh we travelled extensively and experienced a lot of potholes. Can you fill them in one and a quarter month?

YOGI ADITYANATH: Definitely.

Rahul: How will you?

YOGI ADITYANATH: You just see. *(With a confident smile on his face)*

Rahul: But you remember if the potholes are not filled by the 15 June then Aajtak's team will be going around with cameras to check.

YOGI ADITYANATH: You should certainly go. I want you to start this camera drive as soon as possible, as it will create mass awareness. We want the media and people to come forward and participate in the development of Uttar Pradesh. I cannot go everywhere, both my Deputy Chief Ministers, my Ministers and MLAs cannot cover all the roads. I gather news every day from different channels and in the evening ask for updates from the related departments. We take action on any serious stories covered by media. I will be very happy, to get feedback through media, about the places and instances where work is not being done.

(Channel's Anchor Rahul takes people's feedback on Yogi government's performance from a field correspondent in Gorakhpur)

Rahul: Yogi ji, on your home turf in Gorakhpur, people are giving you full marks, as they love you. But there are many other issues like this anti-Romeo Squad thing has come up. Though I understand that women's security is very important, but there are instances where husband-wife, girlfriend-boyfriend, brother-sister were together and police punished them too. So how will you stop this?

YOGI ADITYANATH: See anti-Romeo Squad is essential in Uttar Pradesh and it will work in future also. At the time of constituting the anti-Romeo Squad we made clear guidelines. I have clearly instructed that anti-Romeo Squad will work on the roadside-Romeos and if two friends are sitting or walking together with mutual consent, they will not be disturbed.

The modus operandi of anti-Romeo squad is as follows – our women police will watch the situation near girl's colleges and near other public places and policemen will also be available in the vicinity. If any boy disturbs or harasses any girl, then the anti-Romeo squad will take action. See, we have noticed around 15000 cases in all over Uttar Pradesh, and out of which 14000 people were handed over to their guardians, 500 people were left with a warning and in 500 cases we have taken stricter action.

We realized the seriousness of this problem during the election campaign. Whenever we went around visiting different places and meeting people, girls always mentioned the menace of being troubled and disturbed by the men while going to schools and colleges. So the idea of 'anti-Romeo Squad' came into being. The police may have made a few mistakes and whosoever has gone beyond the guidelines of anti-Romeo squad, have had strict actions against them by their seniors.

Rahul: Many people have sent their questions for you through Facebook and Twitter. Shaba Mustafah has asked that the builders in Uttar Pradesh specially in NCR region have taken lakhs of money from common people and they are not delivering on the promises. What will Yogi Adityanath do against them?

YOGI ADITYANATH: Real estate regulation act is implemented in Uttar Pradesh and it will be effective from the 1 May. We have also appointed an authority for the same and very soon we are going to announce the regulations. Buyers from Noida and Greater Noida have already come to me to with this problem and I have asked my officials to discuss it with the real state companies. Companies should comply with the agreements and promised dates and if the companies have any administrative issues, they can talk to the government. But if they don't comply, government will naturally work against them.

(Channel's Anchor Rahul takes people's feedback on Yogi government's performance through field correspondent in Varanasi)

Rahul: *(Referring to a field question)*. This is a pertinent question- you are telling the police force to stop corruption and be on time, but they have a long-standing reputation of being corrupt and ineffective. Do you think it will stop just by you telling them to stop?

YOGI ADITYANATH: There will be a change and I'm sure the change is already showing. I think more than seeing the change one should feel it. Secondly there are many new appointments in the police force that need to be made in Uttar Pradesh. Because of blatant discrepancies in police selection, the Honorable Supreme Court has stayed the selection process. We have presented our new representation in the Supreme Court (SC) and as soon as it has cleared, we will appoint 130000 police personnel in Uttar Pradesh through a completely transparent system. These new police officers will join us soon, and will strengthen the law and order in the state. I am glad that judiciary is helping us to expedite the process. SC did not agree to resume the recruitment in previous government, as the court was suspicious of their working style. But now court has agreed. In first phase, we are going to appoint 30000 police constables and sub-Inspectors.

Rahul: Next question is coming through Facebook. Manish Kumar has asked, that on one side there are successful businessmen like Baba Ramdev, whose company is growing very fast and in politics it is you. So the time has come when people have started believing that if you want to make your child successful, make them a Yogi.

YOGI ADITYANATH: This is a very good question. I am very concerned myself that the tradition of saints and yogis is rapidly decreasing in this country. So if every family sends one of its members with us then we will fill the gap. We have various examples to go by. We have Prime Minister Narendra Modi, who is working tirelessly as a yogi for the development and prosperity of the country. Baba Ramdev has changed the way *sanyaas*(Sainthood) is being looked at. *Sanyaas* doesn't mean to beg. It's a matter of self-reliance and self-dependence and Baba Ramdev has set a good example for the society through his work. My party has given me a chance to lead Uttar Pradesh and for the benefit Uttar Pradesh we will do whatever is required.

Rahul: After you became the Chief Minister, this is the first time we are interviewing you. But before this I have interviewed you for *'Seedhi Baat'* a couple of times. But the Yogi of *'Seedhi baat'* days and the Yogi Adityanath of today are two very different people. That Yogi was very aggressive, but now you are sitting relaxed and smiling. Yogi Ji, you seem to have changed a lot.

YOGI ADITYANATH: Look, I have not changed. I am the same as I was before. My working style is same as it was earlier. Before I thought about Gorakhpur, but now I am thinking about the whole State of Uttar Pradesh. Naturally I am working as per the responsibility given to me by the party. Some time aggression is required and sometime its not. We have gone hard on criminals. Do you think that's possible without aggression? A few people did not like the idea of anti- Romeo Squad and the shutting down of illegal slaughterhouses. But we firmly executed them for the benefit of the people and that's not possible without aggression.

Rahul: During the campaign, you were one of the most popular faces of the party. So were you expecting that if party wins, you will be a deserving Chief Minister candidate?

YOGI ADITYANATH: I never thought about this and I never longed for something like this. Our national president gave us multiple responsibilities during the elections. He guided us on how to work in different areas and in different situations. During assembly elections we worked in many regions of Uttar Pradesh and also of other states. It has been very hectic for the past three months and so I wanted to take a break for a week. And fortunately I got a timely chance too. I got a call from our Minister for External Affairs (MEA), Sushma Swaraj Ji on 4 or 5 March. She told that there is a program at the Port of Spain and asked for my availability. I thought that the campaigning would finish on the 6 March and after that I can go. I applied for my visa. My passport was submitted. But PMO returned my passport. On the 10 March an official from the MEA's office informed me that some other member of parliament will go for the program. I was little disappointed.

I felt that I got the chance to travel in such delegations three times in the past and two of which I denied myself. On the same day, while coming back to Gorakhpur, I got a call from the External Affairs Minister saying that PMO denied my travel as the Prime Minister felt that I will be needed tomorrow, after the Uttar Pradesh assembly results are declared. I came back to Gorakhpur for *Holi* celebrations and then returned to Delhi for party meetings. After the results were declared I didn't meet any of the party members. At around 10:15 AM, on the request of Amit Shah Ji, I went to see him and we had a general discussion over poll results and I returned to Gorakhpur. In the evening Amit Ji called again and when he realized that I was in Gorakhpur, he arranged for a charter flight the very next morning and I came to Delhi and met him again. He told me to go to Lucknow to take oath as the Chief Minister of Uttar Pradesh. I hadn't come prepared and I had just one pair of clothes. Just a day before I had a discussion with Amit Ji and he did not mention anything then. I was in dilemma whether to go to Lucknow or to Gorakhpur. Amit ji asked me to leave for Lucknow and I did that. In the evening the newly elected members of the Legislative Assembly chose me as their Chief Minister and the next day I took oath. So this is what has happened. But I never desired nor asked for anything.

Rahul: Amazing.

(Channel's Anchor Rahul takes people's feedback on Yogi government's performance through field correspondent at Lucknow)

Rahul: Some of these questions sound very important. The first one was from where we will get the money to implement all the schemes you have spoken about? Uttar Pradesh has a loan of rupees 70,000 Crores. You don't have money. Recently you have waived off farmers' loans worth rupees 37000 Crores. You want to make roads, industries and want to waive off the loans. Yogi Ji from where you will get the money?

YOGI ADITYANATH: We have arranged for the money and I believe that if Baba Ramdev can have an annual business of 10000 crores then I can also work hard and change the image of Uttar Pradesh. We have stopped our unnecessary expenditures.

Rahul: Which ones do you think are unnecessary?

YOGI ADITYANATH: Everything that is meant for show-off and pompous display of power is unnecessary. But I don't wish to make it public because it will be a matter of futile gossip. We not only have the burden of farmer loan waivers, but after the seventh pay commission we also have the burden of extra 30,000 crores for increased salaries. I can firmly say that by keeping a check on unnecessary expenditures, we will save around 12,000 crores to 15,000 crores per year. Moreover, we can also save money by curbing corruption. We will disburse additional loans in the next two years. We will keep coming up with more welfare schemes. We will constantly work for the betterment of the basic amenities like road, health, law and order etc. We will never let anyone feel that the state is burdened with the pressure of farmer's loan waiver. No extra tax will be levied to make up for the farmer's loan waiver. Government will manage resources by checking on its unnecessary expenditure.

In another interview on India TV[25], talking on the same topic Yogi said that, we have cut all the summer foreign trips of the Ministers and bureaucrats, made in the name of study tours. This summer, all my Ministers and officials are out of their comfort zones, on the field, overseeing roads, schools, hospitals and facing the heat along with the public of Uttar Pradesh.

Rahul: The second question was related to cows. You want to stop cow slaughter. But a cow becomes a liability for the poor farmer, once it stops giving milk. It costs Rs 60 per day

25 https://www.youtube.com/watch?v=xshgEQfGca4&t=3s

to rear a cow. It will cost around one lakh crore, to take care of all the cows of the state.

YOGI ADITYANATH: In Uttar Pradesh, '*Gau Sewa Aayog*' is already working. In Bundelkhand region, this has become a trend to leave cows on roads after milking them. You can find hundreds of cows roaming on roads in Bundelkhand. We are planning to create large sheds for such cows with the support of NGOs, trusts and other social organizations.

Rahul: Yogi Ji, let's discuss about the crime that's happening in the name of cows? On our channel we ran 'Operation Gow Rakshak' part-2, in which we have shown that how the people who call themselves *Gow Rakshaks(saviors of cows)*, confessed that they beat the cows, break their legs, break their bones, but make sure that they don't bleed. How will you stop it?

YOGI ADITYANATH: Cow is sacred in Hinduism and has many religious believes attached to it. We are determined to stop smuggling of cows and we will stop it completely. We will also not allow anyone to take law in his or her own hands. If *Gaurakshaks* find a problem, they should report it to police and police will act on it with all sincerity. All *Gaurakshaks* are not aggressive and many of them are doing brilliant work. Let's not quote only the negative examples.

RAHUL: Well said! This should happen. If anyone goes against the law then strict action should be taken against him or her.

(Channel's Anchor Rahul takes people's feedback on Yogi government's performance through field correspondent at Muzaffarnagar.)

RAHUL: People look at your old comments and ask whether minorities have any place in 'Yogi Raj'? Do they need to live as second-class citizens? So what do you want to say to those people who think that the secular balance of the state will change due to Yogi Adityanath?

YOGI ADITYANATH: There were similar issues raised when Modi Ji became the Prime Minister of the country. Do any of those people face any difficulty in Modi's government now? We all have joined here for a mission, and there is no place for any partiality. We will give security to everyone and we will work for everybody's development. But if anyone is thinking that we will work like the previous governments then they are mistaken. No partiality will be done on the basis of '*Teeka*' (Hindu symbol on the forehead) or '*Topi*' (skull cap). Whoever wants to sport a *Teeka,* certainly can and whoever wants to put a *Topi* may do so as well. But if anyone thinks that government will be lenient on the basis of *Teeka* or *Topi,* then it's impossible. We will work on the concept of *'Sabka Saath Sabka Vikas'* that our Prime Minister gave us. Our government has an icon to follow, our Honorable Prime Minister. We will walk in his footsteps and maintain a robust system in Uttar Pradesh.

RAHUL: Yogi ji, going-forward will you ban alcohol like in Bihar?

YOGI ADITYANATH: After shutting down illegal slaughterhouse many people are asking that what will we eat now? So, is it the government's job to run slaughterhouses? We are now working on this problem and you are giving me a new one. Let it be the way it is as of now. We will take the right step at the right moment, in the interest of the state.

Rahul: Okay Yogi Ji, last question before we end our discussion. Samajvadi government was often blamed for protecting the violators of law and for treating criminals as VIPs. Recently we observed that people, who claim to be your supporters, broke the law. People are upset about this. Questions are being raised, that are your so-called supporters allowed to break law?

YOGI ADITYANATH: Not at all. Whosoever tries to take the law in their hands, will be punished. We are working against them and we will continue to work against them. I would also like to warn all those people who are attempting to destroy the image of Bhartiya Janta Party and other Hindu organizations. We have stated it earlier also that Uttar Pradesh will run on rule of law and we will not forgive anyone who tries to break it.

Rahul: Yogi ji, one thing is said about Uttar Pradesh that till the time Uttar Pradesh does not develop, the whole country will lag behind. In such a scenario, everybody expects that you can convert Uttar Pradesh- from an '*Ulta Pradesh*' to an '*Uttam Pradesh*'. You shared a lot of things, ideas and plans. You have set a big target for yourself. We will keep a watch on the developments of Uttar Pradesh. You have many well-wishers for your mission. Thanks a lot for the time and for answering our questions.

War of words between CM Yogi and Nitish Kumar

On 14 June, on the eve of Yogi Adityanath's Darbhanga visit, Chief Minster of Bihar, Nitish Kumar, challenged his Uttar Pradesh counterpart Yogi Adityanath, not to come 'empty handed' but implement the liqour ban and 50 per cent reservation for women in local bodies[26].

On 15th June, responding to the Bihar CM's poser on if the UP government would announce 50 per cent reservation for women, Adityanath said: "Nitish Kumar loves talking about 'aadhi aawadi (women)", but why is he silent on triple talaq?… the silence of secular (brigade) on triple talaq reflects difference in its actions and words"[27]. IN HIS first visit to Bihar after taking over as Uttar Pradesh Chief Minister, Yogi Adityanath dared his Bihar counterpart Nitish Kumar to close down illegal slaughterhouses in the state within 24 hours

26 http://zeenews.india.com/bihar/nitish-kumar-asks-up-counterpart-yogi-adityanath-to-not-come-to-bihar-empty-hand-2015358.html

27 http://indianexpress.com/article/india/in-bihar-yogi-adityanath-dares-nitish-kumar-to-close-illegal-slaughterhouses/

as he did in UP. Responding to Kumar's poser on imposing prohibition in UP, he said that if people of Bihar followed Yoga strictly, there would be no need for prohibition, reported Santosh Singh of Indian Express[28]. Adityanath was speaking about the NDA government's achievements in the past three years at a gathering in Darbhanga, where Nitish addressed a public meeting a day before.

Political pundits are not taking this war of words as a usual incident. Sunita Aron of Hindustan Times[29] wrote that the new rising star of the party, Yogi can easily cut through the caste equations of the Grand Alliance and can turn the tables in favor of BJP in 2019. Political observer Prof Rajesh Singh says the BJP needed a fresh face to match the stature of Bihar's two regional satraps – CM Nitish Kumar and RJD chief Lalu Prasad. Yogi fills that vacuum. The saffron-robed Yogi still carries the aura of a Mahant, which blurs his Rajput caste and charms both the backwards and the forwards. Political expert HV Shahi says Yogi's deployment in Bihar will help in two ways. First, Yogi will have traction for the forward castes that somehow cannot relate to Sushil Modi. Second, Yogi will be able to reach out to the OBCs, break their hegemony that had hurt the BJP's prospects in the assembly elections.

Face-off between Yogi Sarkar and Rahul Gandhi

Yogi government presented its first budget on 11th July in the Uttar Pradesh Assembly. A section of media reported[30] that, Rs 576 Cr had been allotted for secondary education in this budget against Rs 9990 Cr last year and only Rs 272 Cr for higher education compared to Rs 2742 Cr allotted

28 http://indianexpress.com/article/india/in-bihar-yogi-adityanath-dares-nitish-kumar-to-close-illegal-slaughterhouses/

29 http://www.hindustantimes.com/analysis/why-up-cm-yogi-adityanath-could-do-the-trick-for-the-bjp-in-bihar-2019/story-Pga85xzgTiDFfm7CxDGy0N.html

30 http://www.business-standard.com/article/economy-policy/yogi-s-up-budget-education-funds-slashed-akhilesh-laptops-go-to-junkyard-117071101392_1.html

last year. Quoting this news report, Congress Vice-President Rahul Gandhi had tweeted - "Great move CM Yogi - next you can save more money by closing all the hospitals,". The Yogi Adityanath government contested Rahul Gandhi's jibe that the UP government has massively cut education funds in its recent budget. The funds have in fact been increased by almost 25% in the present budget, UP government has said[31].

Aman Sharma of ET reported that, Uttar Pradesh deputy Chief Minister and education minister Dinesh Sharma said figures of slashing down education budget in some news reports were completely wrong and the government had paid full attention to education. The Chief Minister's Office has also issued a statement saying the total budget for education (basic, secondary and higher education) in the present budget has risen by 25.4% from Rs 49607 Cr last year to Rs 62185 Cr. "The budget for basic education has increased from Rs 38066 Cr last year to Rs 50142 Cr. The budget for secondary education has increased from Rs 8956 Cr last year to Rs 9384 Cr and budget for higher education has increased from 2585 Cr last year to Rs 2655 Cr," the UP government said in a statement, pointing to its official budget document.

31 http://economictimes.indiatimes.com/articleshow/59620960.cms?utm_source=contentofinterest&utm_medium=text&utm_campaign=cppst

Section 2.
Yogi Adityanath, five time Member of Parliament from Gorakhpur

As per norms, the Chief Minister and Ministers, who are not members of the State Legislature, are required to become members of either House of legislature, within six months of taking the oath as a Chief Minister or minister. It is still not clear if Adityanath would prefer to be elected to the Assembly or follow the example of his predecessors, Akhilesh Yadav and Mayawati, both of whom preferred to be MLCs rather than become MLAs[32].

On 21 March, two days after taking the oath as the CM of UP, Yogi Adityanath attended the budget session of the Parliament. While participating in the budget debate, he also delivered his farewell speech, on the Lok Sabha floor.

Yogi's farewell speech in the parliament

"........Madam Speaker, I am thankful to you for providing me an opportunity to speak on the Finance Bill. I am also thankful to the leader of my party and the Prime Minister of the country, Honorable Narendra Modi. I am also thankful to the Parliamentary Affairs Minister Shri Anant Kumar, who gave me a chance to speak on this important topic on

32 http://www.hindustantimes.com/lucknow/many-bjp-lawmakers-from-east-up-offer-to-vacate-their-seats-for-yogi/story-7RuUAwKce5HtLJmRl4mrFL.html

behalf of my party. Madam, Narendra Modi's government inherited a limping economy, an economy with decreasing growth rate along with an environment of distrust around the country. With extreme courage and determination, the Modi government has established a government dedicated to the welfare of the people, a government determined to have good governance and a government working towards increasing the growth rate of the country. Because of this, he has become a role model not only in India, but in all the democratically ruled countries of the world. That's why where ever we have elections around the globe; global leaders are putting forth our Prime Minister Shri Narendra Modi as their icon. People now want to see and understand from India the structure for an ideal development.

In 2014 the new government had extremely adverse conditions. Fiscal deficit was at 8.9 percent of the GDP, revenue deficit was at 2.8 percent of the GDP, inflation was hovering at 11.2 percent, and the current account deficit was 4.6 per cent of the GDP. Under such circumstances our glorious Prime Minister Shri Narendra Modi Ji held the government, and for the last 3 years this government has successfully raised the growth rate of the country to around 8 percent to 8.5 per cent. After demonetization everyone was curious of the consequences but despite demonetization, the growth rate has been higher than 7.9 per cent. The world is surprised that a developing economy like India is doing so well and for that I congratulate our Honorable Finance Minister who successfully gave a new life to the economy. Apart from the revival of the economy, during the same interval, a number of welfare schemes were also announced and executed. I would like to throw some light on some of these policies, as some members always create doubt that these polices existed, even before 2014.

During elections and post-elections speeches, Honorable Prime Minister mentioned with full conviction that his government would be devoted to help the farmers and needy without any bias of caste, creed or religion. Madam! I still remember in 1996-98 during a national disaster period, I got the opportunity to visit the affected farmers. I observed that government distributed the cheques of Rs 1000 to the farmers. But most of the farmers did not have bank accounts then. The banks asked the farmers to deposit Rs 500 first as the minimum balance to open the account and only then their cheques could be deposited. No other government until now had thought about this, but with the help of *Jan Dhan Yojna* the government helped in opening the bank accounts for more than 25 crores needy people and their families. This shows the positive inclination of this government towards the poor. This scheme (*Jan Dhan Yojna*) is open for every common man, from any caste or religion. The schemes, which were announced subsequently, whether it was the Digital India, or StandUp India, are for the enlightenment of the youth. For empowering the youth, government also started *'Pradhan Mantri Mudra Bank Yojna'*. A wonderful scheme call *'Pradhan Mantri Ujjawa Yojna'* was started for the wellbeing of rural women. During one of our rural visits a woman told us that now she has no fear if she doesn't get firewood to cook as now our Prime Minister has sent the LPG cylinder through *Ujjwal Yojna*.

As we are discussing the finance bill, we all know that the eastern parts of our country are always been ignored and are highly underdeveloped. I am getting elected to this House from Eastern Uttar Pradesh, since 1998, and every time I shared the problems of Eastern UP, in the house, no one bothered. For the last 26 years the fertilizer factory of Gorakhpur has been closed and whenever I shared my thoughts on it, I got replies like, 'We will make some policies' or 'How can we start the closed industries?'. Now I thank our Prime Minister who not only has re-opened the closed factory, but also ensured that work also began there. Before 2019 Barauni and Sindri fertilizers factories will also be established in Gorakhpur.

I had strongly demanded attention many a times, in the House, to the 34 districts of Eastern Uttar Pradesh that are affected by encephalitis and to the children who were losing their lives because of it. I was surprised that those who talk about minorities, lower castes and disadvantaged communities never uttered a word about the death of these innocent children. More than 90 percent of the children, who die every year due to encephalitis, are from the minorities and the lower castes. Nobody has ever tried to reach out to them. Now Honorable Prime Minister has given Gorakhpur the best medical organization of India – All India Institute of Medical Sciences (AIIMS) that will start its operations soon.

The model for development for rural India was given by our respected Former Prime Minister Shri Atal Bihari Vajpayee, in the form of *'Pradhan Mantri Gramin Sadak Yojna'*. He also gave the model for the multi-lane national expressways. In Modi government, the work on all of these has re-started at a good pace.

Madam Speaker, since 1998, I have learnt a lot of things about the parliamentary systems in this House. My party has given me the responsibility of Uttar Pradesh and I am fully committed to render my services for the state. In last two and half years more than 2.5 lac crores has been given to Uttar Pradesh by the Modi government, but unfortunately only 78 thousand crores has not been utilized as the former government did not have any development structure.

The mandate given by the people of Uttar Pradesh is a tight slap on opposition's face. Madam Speaker, in Uttar Pradesh we will establish a robust government under the guidance of the Honorable Prime Minister. Our government will have an inclusive development structure under the *'Sabka Saath Sabka Vikas'* theme. We will take the resolution to work for every caste, religion, and category. We will work for every citizen and for the development of every area. We will use the budget unspent until now, for the development of the state.

When I first came to this House in 1998, I was a thin, young boy of just 26 years and I still remember the condition of Gorakhpur at the time. There is an incident from then that I would like to share with you all. I had gotten the opportunity to meet with the then Minister for Fertilizer and Chemical, Mr. Surjeet Singh Barnala. When I met him, he stared at me continuously for long time and asked if I was elected from Gorakhpur. When I confirmed that I was, he asked again if I was from Gorakhpur. To which I replied yes. He asked for the third time if I was actually elected from Gorakhpur and I reconfirmed it to him and enquired why he was asking me this so many times. He said that he had once visited Gorakhpur for an election rally, but as bombs were being thrown from both the sides, he ran away from the place and has never visited Gorakhpur again. This was the image of Gorakhpur. I was stunned and ashamed to hear the perception people had of my city. I went back to Gorakhpur and called the local businesses and social organizations and narrated this shameful incident. I called upon everyone to work towards changing this image. Madam Speaker, but I can say with confidence that for the last 15 years, no businessman has had to pay '*gunda* tax' (tax levied by local goons) in Gorakhpur, not a single businessman or doctor was kidnapped and we have never allowed anyone to spread chaos in the city. Unfortunately, what we used to hear about Gorakhpur fifteen years ago is what we are hearing about the whole of Uttar Pradesh now. In the last 5 Year Uttar Pradesh has faced many riots, but none of them have happened in Eastern Uttar Pradesh and now I assure the House that without a doubt we will make the whole of Uttar Pradesh riots free and crime free.

People often talk about my age. I am one year younger than respected Rahul ji and one year older than Mr. Akhilesh Yadav. I came in between both of them and I guess this is the reason of their failure *(house breaks into laughter)*, but I will invite every one of you to Uttar Pradesh. You all have given me a lot of love and affection. I have learnt a lot of things from this House. In fact, manners and behavior can be learnt from this House. I was nervous and skeptical of everyone's behavior when I was elected the first time. But as soon as I entered the premises of the parliament I observed a totally different level of kindness from every single member and every single employee here. This should be told to the people, as a very different image has been created outside.

Inside the house, we all debate, argue and are loud. That is a part of democracy, but when we meet in the gallery, we greet and hug each other. We leave all our differences here and meet everyone outside with dignity.

My party leaders have given me the responsibility of Uttar Pradesh and I invite every one of you to come there. Uttar Pradesh welcomes you with open arms. Our beloved Prime Minister was also elected from Uttar Pradesh and soon it will be one of the best states of the country, a state free from corruption and chaos. Many things will stop in Uttar Pradesh, mothers and sisters will never face a situation that will require them to appeal anywhere. We will provide such a robust development model to Uttar Pradesh that the youth will not have to migrate anywhere. I invite the whole House to Uttar Pradesh.

"Madam Speaker, you have given all of us so much affection in this house. You have always handled this house efficiently and provided opportunities to all the new comers to grow and I thank you for that. The dreams of our Honorable Prime Minister for Uttar Pradesh, for its development, will soon be a reality. With this, I thank you all.",

His speech had some humor, some satire and interesting anecdotes. He narrated his journey as a parliamentarian, his work in Gorakhpur over last two decades, his deep belief in the Parliamentary system, his bonding with fellow members, the current state of Uttar Pradesh and inspiration that he draws from the grand vision of ex-Prime Minister Atal Bihari Vajpayee and current Prime Minister Narendra Modi. It was a pleasure for everyone to hear a very different and composed Yogi Adityanath.

Electoral story of Gorakhpur Lok Sabha seat

Yogi's tryst with politics began in 1996, when he was named in-charge of managing the election campaign for Mahant Avaidyanath. In 1998, when Avaidyanath retired from active politics, he declared Yogi as his nominee for the next Lok

Sabha polls. Adityanath has been winning the Gorakhpur seat since 1998; at 26, he was the youngest MP in the 12 Lok Sabha. Gorakhpur district and Lok Sabha area is very important in Yogi Adityanath's rise in politics. Gorakhpur has a long history of prestigious and interesting electoral contests.

Mahant Digvijaynath and Mutt's first representation in Lok Sabha

Gorakhpur is one of the very important Lok Sabha seats in eastern Uttar Pradesh, which sets the tone of the voters in that part of the state. Shri Sinhasan Singh, of Indian National Congress (INC) held Gorakhpur seat from the very first general elections of 1952 until 1967. In 1967, Mahant Digvijaynath, head priest, of the Gorakhnath Mutt, a Hindu nationalist, an activist and a politician of the Hindu Mahasabha contested for the seat as an independent candidate and won the seat by a margin of more than 42700 votes against Shri S.L. Saxena of Indian National Congress. It was said that Mahant Digvijaynath played a leading role in the *Ram Janmabhoomi* movement in 1949, which culminated in the placing of lord *Rama* idols inside the Babri Masjid. Gorakhnath Mutt has always had a considerable influence in the local and regional politics, but this was the first time, someone from the Mutt ever engaged in the formal political process.

An orphan from Udaipur and a Rajput by caste, Digvijaynath, the Mahant of the Gorakhnath temple was born in 1894 and was brought up in the Mutt. He joined the Congress in 1921 and was arrested for taking an active part in the Chauri Chaura incident. He joined the Hindu Mahasabha in 1937, when Savarkar took over, 3 years after being appointed as the Mahant, and soon became head of the party's unit in the United Provinces (now Uttar Pradesh). Like many members of the Mahasabha, he strongly opposed Mahatma Gandhi. Many alleged that just three days before Gandhi's murder, he had provoked many Hindu nationalists against Mahatama Gandhi's wrong decision of favoring the formation of Pakistan[33]. He was subsequently arrested, along with Professor Ram Singh and VG Deshpande, but released after 9 months due to the absence of any substantial evidence. His status as the Mahant of the Gorakhnath Mutt as well as his political acumen helped him rise fast. He was a Hindu nationalist known for his beliefs that the Muslims should prove their loyalty to India, if they wanted to be part of this country.

Mahant Avaidyanath, first MLA from the Mutt

In 1940, Mahant Avaidyanath came in contact of Mahant Digvijaynath and by 1942 he became the successor of Gorakhshdham Peeth (*aka Gorakhnath Mutt*). Though the Mutt always had a considerable influence in socio-political affairs of the region, Mahant Avaidyanath was the first one from the Mutt to run for a political office and become the Member of Legislative Assembly (MLA) of Uttar Pradesh. Avaidyanath got elected as an MLA from the Maniram Assembly segment five times in 1962, 1967, 1968 1974 and 1977. In 1962, he contested from Maniram Assembly seat of Gorakhpur on Hindu Mahasabha ticket, against Shri Keshav Pande of Indian National Congress (INC) and defeated him by a margin of 17664 votes. Maniram seat came into existence only in 1962 and Mahant Avaidyanath became the first MLA to represent it. In 1967, he contested on the same seat as an independent candidate and won it. He contested from the same Maniram Assembly constituency again in 1969 and 1974 on the Hindu Mahasabha ticket and won the seat. He retained the seat even in the year 1977 on Janta Party ticket, in the first post-emergency elections.

When Mahant Avaidyanath's guru Mahant Digvijaynath died in 1969, he was the Member of Parliament from Gorakhpur Lok Sabha constituency. In the by-elections in the year 1970 Mahant Avaidyanath contested from his guru's constituency and won as an independent candidate. He won from the same Lok Sabha seat again in 1989 as candidate of

33 Krishna and Dhirendra K. Jha (Ayodhya: The Dark Night, page 28).

Hindu Mahasabha. In 1991 and 1996 general elections, he won the same seat as a Bhartiya Janata Party candidate.

Yogi Adityanath, building on the political legacy of the Mutt

Yogi Adityanath completed his graduation in science from Uttarakhand. In 1994, at 22, he was initiated into the *Nath Panth* by his guru Mahant Avaidyanath, who was the head priest at Gorakhnath Mutt then. Those were the years when Purvanchal was trying to slip out from the grips of musclemen politicians Harishankar Tiwari and Virendra Pratap Shahi. Yogi played a strong role to end the musclemen culture in the region. Yogi Adityanath appealed to the imagination of students and young population of Gorakhpur. They saw him as a successor of Mahant Digvijaynath, who was from Gorakhpur and remembered for the pivotal role he had played in the Chauri Chaura incident of 1921, which forced Mahatma Gandhi to call off his non-cooperation movement. Yogi Adityanath's popularity soared further when his guru anointed him as his formal successor of the Gorakhnath Mutt, which he now heads after the demise of Mahant Avaidyanath in 2014.

With the blessings of Avaidyanath and riding on his influence in Gorakhpur, Yogi Adityanath contested in the Lok Sabha elections in 1998 and got elected for the first time with a margin of over 26,000 votes. In 1998, Adityanath was the youngest member of the 12 Lok Sabha at just 26. Yogi Adityanath has never lost an election since then. The Runners up from Gorakhpur Lok Sabha kept changing, but Yogi's vote percentage and winning margin kept increasing, barring in 1999 when his winning margin was hardly 7000 votes against Samajwadi Party's (SP) Jamuna Prasad Nishad. In 2004, when Bhartiya Janta Party performed poorly, Yogi still managed to win his seat with a margin of 1 lac 40 thousand votes against the same Jamuna Prasad Nishad of SP. In 2009, the victory margin for Yogi became, 2 lac 20 thousand votes, against, Vinay Shankar Tiwari of Bahujan Samaj Party (BSP). Vinay Shankar Tiwari is the son of famous muscleman of the eastern region, Hari Shankar Tiwari. Popular Bhojpuri singer, Manoj Tiwari, also tried his hands in politics for the first time, against Yogi Adityanath, when he contested the Lok Sabha elections from Gorakhpur on SP's ticket in 2009 and stood third with 83,000 votes. Manoj Tiwari later joined BJP and is now the State President of BJP, Delhi and Member of Parliament of BJP from North-East Delhi since 2014. Yogi won his seat with sweeping margins in 2004 and 2009, when BJP got disappointing results nationally. In 2014's Modi-wave, Yogi won Gorakhpur seat again, with an over whelming margin of over 3 lac votes against Rajmati Nishad of SP.

Over the years, Yogi has made a very strong people and political connect in Gorakhpur and brand Yogi has become a cult with each passing day. Soon every nook and corner of Gorakhpur was chanting – '*Gorakhpur mein rehna hai to Yogi Yogi kehna hai!*' (If you want to live in Gorakhpur, you have to chant Yogi's name).

Yogi's *Janta Darbar* at the Mutt

Pradeep Rao, a close associate of Yogi Adityanath in Gorakhpur, told me that three things that makes Yogi, a mass leader are – him being the head priest of such an important ancient Mutt, the presence of people from all castes and religions among his co-workers at the Mutt and most importantly his '*vyapakjan sampark*' (massive people connect). His connection to the people is not through *karykartas* (volunteers), party-workers or associates of the Mutt. He has a direct connect with the people. For the last two decades, he has strengthened the legacy of his *guru*, Mahant Avaidyanath, of having *Janta Darbars* (meeting people for grievance redressal). He dedicates quality hours per day at the Mutt, to listen to people's problems. People not only from Gorakhpur, but also from others districts of Uttar Pradesh, especially eastern UP, come to Yogi's *darbar*, when they lose hope from every quarter. People come with various requests, ranging from getting their railway tickets confirmed, to getting their pension and scholarship transfer sorted, getting medical treatment in good government facilities, to when police is not helping them against the musclemen. Yogi's Janta Darbar at the Mutt is a busy indigenous styled office, where phones keep ringing with requests, noisy typewriters keep chattering with drafting cover letters to help the applicants. This help is offered irrespective of the applicant's class, caste or religion.

As reported by India TV[34], Abdul, an applicant who came to Yogi's *darbar for* his wife, as she had some serious complications in her kidney. Abdul quickly got a letter of reference on Yogi's letterhead, to get admitted in KGMC, Lucknow, which is one of the premium hospitals in the state capital. People say that letter from the Mutt is like a magic wand, which cuts through the red-tapism of the government machinery and gets work done.

The way it works is, first the office of Yogi at the Mutt scans through the problem and gives a reference letter for the genuine requests. Yogi personally attends many of the applicants and hears their problems. If the applicant returns with the plea that an officer is not honoring the letter, the officer immediately gets a call from the Mutt and many times it is from Yogi himself. If the call also does not work, which is very rare, Yogi reaches the respective office. When this popular and beloved leader of Gorakhpur, reaches any government office, thousands join him on the way and then the officer is forced to attend to the request of the applicant. With several precedents of such *gheraos* and protests, now the letter or a call from the Mutt is enough to get the work done.

Mr Rao also told me that even when any influential person comes with some powerful reference in Yogi's *darbar*, he still attends first to the distressed and disadvantaged, as he believes that powerful ones will somehow get their things done, but the weak only have Baba Gorakhnath for

34 Magic Letter That Gets All Work Done In Yogi Adityanath's Gorakhpur Durbar https://www.youtube.com/watch?v=Y0hhHXbEJfI

assistance. I was told that Yogi feels that if he does not help the needy, then God will not excuse him.

In 2017, power structures have changed. Now Yogi Adityanath is the Chief Minister of the state. Yogi is still continuing the *janta darbar* at 5, Kalidas Marg in Lucknow[35]. The only difference now is that the letter goes from the CM Office and it does not need a follow up call or a protest for resolution. While Yogi is away in Lucknow, the *janta darbar* at the Mutt still continues. Yogi's close associate Dwarka Prasad Tiwari holds the fort and monitors the speedy resolution of grievances at the Mutt. It seems like soon there will be a formal mini Chief Minister Office (CMO) in Gorakhpur just like the Prime Minister's Office (PMO) in Varanasi.

Inspired by Yogi's *janta darbar*, BJP has started a similar arrangement in the state party office, where Ministers take turns and listen to the problems of the commoners.

With strong people-connect Yogi has built a very strong base in Gorakhpur and in the entire eastern belt of Uttar Pradesh. While working very closely with the people in his constituency, Yogi Adityanath also played a very active role as a legislature in the parliament.

Yogi Adityanath, an active parliamentarian

Yogi entered the lower House of the Parliament, the Lok Sabha, very early in his life. From being the member of 12 Lok Sabha till his last speech as a parliamentarian in the 16 Lok Sabha, Yogi has been a very active parliamentarian all along. One measures a member of parliament's (MP) performance, based on his or her attendance, debates that an MP has participated in under different rules of the parliament, questions that an MP has asked in the parliament and the private member bills that an MP has introduced in the parliament. Yogi Adityanath's performance is above the national average in almost all these counts. If we take the example of 16 Lok

35 CM Yogi's residence a new citadel for those in trouble http://www.asianage.com/india/politics/230417/cm-yogis-residence-a-new-citadel-for-those-in-trouble.html

Sabha[36], Yogi participated in 57 debates against the national average of 50.6, Yogi asked 306 questions against a national average of 199 and Yogi introduced 3 private member bills, against the national average of 1.5. This data speaks volumes about his engagement in the parliament. If we compare this data, with someone like Rahul Gandhi, a very senior leader of Congress and heir apparent of Gandhi family, we observe that in 16 Lok Sabha Mr. Gandhi[37], participated in only 11 debates, asked zero questions and introduced no private member bills.

If one drills down on the debates[38] that Yogi Adityanath initiated or participated under different rules (*Special Mention, Calling Attentions, Rule-377 etc.*) of the parliament, one will see a very wide range of topics. We see Yogi raising national issues like the undisclosed foreign income and assets, the need to have a Uniform Civil Code in the country, issues related to the non-payment of sugarcane farmers etc, and he is also equally very concerned for eastern regions of Uttar Pradesh and Gorakhpur related issues like, according a status of Central University to the Gorakhpur University and Indian Institute of Technology to Madan Mohan Malaviya University of Technology, the need to establish an AIIMS like institute in Gorakhpur, the need to make *Gorra* and *Ami* rivers in Gorakhpur pollution free, setting up a new unit of Hindustan Fertilizers Corporation Limited in Gorakhpur, providing permanent land *pattas* to *vanya grams* (forest villages) in the forest areas of the eastern Uttar Pradesh, the need to take action against the spread of Encephalitis in the country, especially in eastern Uttar Pradesh, taking suitable measures to prevent annual floods occurring in districts of eastern UP, the inclusion of Bhojpuri language in the eighth schedule of the constitution etc.

The image the mainstream media projects of Yogi Adityanath is very different from how Yogi conducts himself in the parliament and in his constituency over last two decades.

---

36 http://www.prsindia.org/mptrack/yogiadityanath

37 http://www.prsindia.org/mptrack/rahulgandhi

38 http://loksabha.nic.in/

Media has repeatedly thronged us with a few charged up election time speeches of Yogi, but has never shown us the multi-faceted interventions made by him in the parliament. When Yogi spoke for the rights of the Hindu community, the media painted him as a Hindu hardliner. But in my research I meticulously went through the 300+ questions that this so called 'Hindu hardliner' has asked in the 16 Lok Sabha, and observed him asking questions about Human Development Index (HDI), ways to address the problems being faced by UPSE students who are not proficient in English, shortage of skilled human resources in tourism, targets under PMAYG, power generation capacity of the states, conservation of ancient folk tradition and literature, merger of insurance companies, Start-up India aspiration fund, solar energy based dual pump piped water supply scheme, declining wildlife, crop insurance, schools for child labourers, new civil aviation policy, waste management, upgradation of major ports, research on nutrient content in food products, trade deficit with China, use of fertilizers and pesticide in farming, power generation through municipal solid waste, electronic manufacturing cluster, agreements signed in SAARC summit, safety of Indians working abroad, shortage of basic resources in veterinary colleges, safety of nuclear products, cyber espionage, crime against women and children, non-performing assets (NPAs), impact of monsoon on agriculture, global ranking of Indian universities, setting up of *Krishi Vigyan Kendras*, criteria for setting up new IITs and IIMs, Indo-US ties, Indo-Japan ties, exploration of oil and gas, amendments in MCI guidelines, vector-borne diseases, health insurance scheme for the BPL families and the list goes on. But unfortunately the popular media never bothered to show us this aspect of Yogi Adityanath.

Not to miss that Yogi did ask some culturally oriented questions like the need to shut down illegal slaughter houses and stopping open sale of meat in every nook and corner in Uttar Pradesh, which poses a serious health hazard to the public, the exodus of people of the Hindu community in Kairana, the need to have a Uniform Civil Code in the country, request to declare Shrimad Bhagvat Geeta a national book and teach it to all students.

Over his many terms as parliamentarian, Yogi has been the chairperson and a very active member of various parliamentary committees and has been a part of parliamentary delegations to different countries like Cambodia, Malaysia, Nepal, Singapore, Thailand and U.S.A.

These interventions by Yogi have borne fruits for Gorakhpur and eastern UP. In July 2016, Prime Minister Narendra Modi laid the foundation stone for setting up of an All India Institute of Medical Science (AIIMS) in Gorakhpur at an estimated cost of Rs 1011 crores to provide super-specialty healthcare to people of the state and create a large pool of doctors[39]. In the same visit, PM Modi also laid the foundation stone for the revival of a sick fertilizer plant, a move which will create up to 4000 jobs and ensure adequate supply of nutrients to farmers in Uttar Pradesh. The plant belonging to the Fertilizer Corporation India Ltd (FCIL) has been lying idle since 1990s. It would be revived through a Special Purpose Vehicle (SPV) of Public Sector Units (PSUs) at an estimated cost of rupees 6,000 crores.

Positions Held by Yogi Adiyanath in the Parliament[40]

1998	Elected to 12th Lok Sabha
1998-99	Member, Standing Committee on Food, Civil Supplies and Public Distribution and
	Its Sub-Committee-B on Department of Sugar and Edible Oils Distribution
	Member, Consultative Committee, Ministry of Home Affairs

39 http://www.ndtv.com/cities/pm-modi-lays-foundation-stone-for-aiims-in-gorakhpur-1434745

40 http://164.100.47.194/Loksabha/Members/MemberBioprofile.aspx?mpsno=7

1999	Re-elected to 13th Lok Sabha (2nd term)
1999 – 2000	Member, Standing Committee on Food, Civil Supplies and Public Distribution
	Member, Consultative Committee, Ministry of Home Affairs
2004	Re-elected to 14th Lok Sabha (3rd term)
	Member, Committee on Government Assurances
	Member, Standing Committee on External Affairs
	Member, Consultative Committee, Ministry of Home Affairs
2009	Re-elected to 15th Lok Sabha (4th term)
31 Aug. 2009	Member, Standing Committee on Transport, Tourism and Culture
	Member, Consultative Committee, Ministry of Home Affairs
May, 2014	Re-elected to 16th Lok Sabha (5th term)
14 Aug. 2014 – 30 Apr. 2015	Member, Committee on Public Undertakings
1 Sep. 2014 onwards	Member, Standing Committee on Transport, Tourism and Culture
2 Sep. 2014 onwards	Chairperson, Joint Committee on Salaries and Allowances of Members of Parliament.
	Member, Consultative Committee, Ministry of Home Affairs
29 Jan. 2015 onwards	Member, General Purposes Committee

International Media on Yogi

Yogi's rise to the post of Chief Minister of Uttar Pradesh was not missed by international media either. Washington Post[41] wrote, "Modi's party picks Yogi Adityanath, strident Hindu nationalist priest, as leader of India's biggest state". BBC[42] said, "Yogi Adityanath: Uttar Pradesh Chief Minister choice criticized". New York Times[43] said, "Firebrand Hindu Cleric Yogi Adityanath picked as Uttar Pradesh Minister".

On 12th July, New York Times' South Asia bureau chief Ellen Barry wrote an article on the rise of Yogi Adityanath, whose headline on Twitter read, "Head of militant Hindu temple ascends India's political ladder". India Samvad Bureau[44] reported that this is not the first time when New York Times published an ignorant article about India but still everyone was left shell-shocked when it called Uttar Pradesh Chief Minister a militant. As soon as the article grabbed the attention, Twitter users blasted New York Times for calling Yogi- the "head of militant Hindu temple". Ellen Berry gave a lame excuse, that "Militant" as an adjective is quite general, meaning "aggressive" or "forceful," and has no association with terrorism. But After facing a backlash from Twitterati, the editor seems to have changed the headline to "Firebrand Hindu Cleric Ascends India's Political Ladder[45]."

It is unfortunate that the so-called rigorous journalists from the BBCs, New York Times and Washington Posts of the world, just did shallow reporting of translating some Hindi tabloids into English. Not one of them cared to research his

---

41 https://www.washingtonpost.com/news/worldviews/wp/2017/03/19/for-state-leader-modi-taps-firebrand-politician-who-once-advocated-killing-muslims/

42 http://www.bbc.com/news/world-asia-india-39316597

43 https://www.nytimes.com/2017/03/18/world/asia/firebrand-hindu-cleric-yogi-adityanath-picked-as-uttar-pradesh-minister.html?_r=0

44 http://www.indiasamvad.co.in/top-stories/ny-times-calls-yogi-adityanath-head-of-militant-hindu-temple-23091

45 https://www.nytimes.com/2017/07/12/world/asia/india-yogi-adityanath-bjp-modi.html

record as a parliamentarian, the national and international issues he raised in the parliament over two decades and how he conducted himself in his home constituency and why his vote percentage grew exponentially over years.

Yogi and Controversies

Habitual of minority appeasement politics by the Congress party and having created imaginary hatred with saffron clad yogis, in the name of secularism, any bold, strategic and strong move by Yogi Adityanath was presented as a controversy by the popular media. For the first time this biography will unravel the truth behind all those concocted stories.

1999, Panchrukhia case

Yogi's love for people and his earnest desire to solve their issues has often landed him in tricky situations. During my field research the locals told me of a case where a Muslim group removed an old sacred *peepal* tree, to expand the land of a graveyard (*Kabristan*) in a village named Panchrukhia. As the police did not act against it, Yogi intervened and went to the village to plant a new *Peeple* tree. By the time Yogi was about to come out of the village, Samajwadi Party leader Talat Aziz, organized a *sabha (*gathering*)* around the village to communalize the environment. This is the same party hopper Talat Aziz, who contested for the assembly seat from Paniyara, Maharajganj in 2017 assembly elections, on a Congress ticket and lost. While returning from the village, when Yogi's fleet was leaving the venue peacefully, the last vehicle of Yogi's fleet was heavily stoned by the workers from Aziz's group. Yogi, who was in one of the front vehicles, got the news on the phone and decided to return. His aides advised him not to return but Yogi told that he couldn't turn his back on his people who were in trouble. When Yogi reached the venue of Talat Aziz's *sabha*, firing and heavy stone pelting started on Yogi's vehicle. In retaliatory fire a policeman, Satya Prakash Yadav, the assigned security guard of Talat Aziz died of a bullet injury.

Without knowing enough details of the incident, Deputy Inspector General (DIG) of police of the region, RP Singh ordered the arrest of Yogi Adityanath. Field police got a tip-off from their headquarters that the 'culprit' was in a red Tata Sumo vehicle. On all the three barricades to the Gorakhnath temple, police only found their local Member of Parliament, Yogi Adityanath in the red Sumo and not any 'culprit', so they allowed Yogi's cavalcade to pass through and Yogi reached the temple.

In 1999, it was Kalyan Singh lead BJP government in Lucknow. Powerful Ministers from the eastern region of Uttar Pradesh, like Hari Shankar Tiwari and Shiv Pratap Shukla were at the helm of affairs in Lucknow in a BJP led coalition government. But with the advent of Yogi in Gorakhpur in those years the likes of Hari Shankar Tiwari and Shiv Pratap Shukla were losing their base and so were critical of Yogi's brand of politics. Yogi loyalists still feel that Tiwari and Shukla tried for Yogi's arrest in Panchrukhia case. Later Mahant Avaidyanath intervened and the matter was settled at the level of L K Advani, the then Home Minister and Kalyan Singh, the then Chief Minister.

2002, Formation of Hindu YuvaVahini

Yogi Adityanath formed the Hindu Yuva Vahini (HYV) in April, 2002 on the auspicious occasion of *Ramnavmi* (festival associated with the birth of Lord Rama) as a non-governmental, apolitical and purely cultural organization. As per organizations' charter[46] it aims to spread the feeling of nationalism, uphold the interest of Hindus, raise their concerns collectively, work on faith and belief on Hindu-religious text, work on mutual cooperation, and establish an equal and just society. The charter further explains, that by the term '*Hindu*', they mean anyone who believes in Vedic philosophy, Budhism, Jainism, Sikhism, Naga philosophy, or other Hindu cultural philosophies. Hindu also means anyone else, who believes in and respects the holy sound 'OM', who opposes cow-slaughter,

46 http://www.hinduyuvavahini.in/samvidhan.aspx

who believes in reincarnation, who respects India as his or her motherland, fatherland and sacred land and one who has complete belief and trust on Hindu religious text.

The motto statement of HYV in Hindi goes– *'Tera Vaibhav Amar Rahe Maa, Hum Din Char Rahein na Rahein'*, meaning 'Mother (India), we will ensure your glory remains till time immemorial, even if we are short lived'.

Listed objectives[47] of the Hindu Yuva Vahini are as follows:

a) **Re-organizing Hindus** for re-establishing, securing, nurturing, strengthening Hindu religion, society and cultural heritage of Hindustan (India).
b) Developing **equality** in society, by uprooting, ill practices like untouchability, caste-differences in the society, for the integration and mutual goodwill in larger Hindu society.
c) Pave the way for a reputable and honorable **return to Hinduism** and to 'larger Hindu society', for all those, who were forced to leave their Hindu faith due to fear, temptation, coercion or who had left it themselves due to misbehavior of their own people.
d) Legislative attempts to call for the complete **ban on killing of cow-family** of any age and gender. Promoting cow husbandry and raring of cows.
e) Rising above the party politics, awakening the Hinduism-lead, **national-consciousness in all the Hindus.**
f) Take all legal steps to include all those **fellow-countrymen in the mainstream national life**, who have become isolated as they live in villages, forest areas or inaccessible hilly areas.
g) To develop mutual understanding, **cooperation and harmony in all religions** of Hindu society.
h) Provide service and assistance to mothers, sisters and old aged people, who are **victims of harassment** and exploitation or are helpless due to poor health or poverty.
i) Organized and well-planned efforts to eradicate and control **nationwide corruption.**
j) To become a partner in **empowering India** to create a developed and prosperous nation.

---

47 http://www.hinduyuvavahini.in/samvidhan_2.aspx

k) Providing as much opportunity and support as possible at the government or non-government level to make educated **unemployed youth, self-employed or employable.**
l) To establish **mutual co-ordination** among all national and international organizations of the similar ideology.
m) To fulfill any of the above objectives, establish any small or big institutional organization as required. To start printing and publication of literature for all the above objectives and to establish **"Hindu Fund"** to support all the above objectives.

A glance through the twelve objectives and constitution of Hindu Yuva Vahini, gives a fascinating insight into Yogi Adityanath's political acumen and farsightedness. The charter of HYV beautifully combines many philosophies; RSS's vision of a nation based on ancient Hindu culture, a commitment and love for cows, socialist ideas of equality, ideas around helping the last person in the row, in line with *Deen Dyal Upadhayaji*'s ideas of *Antodaya*, modern ideas of empowering India and generating employment, in line with ideas of Prime Minister Narendra Modi, new age reformist ideas like eradicating corruption and most important ideas around designing required organizational setup, funds, communication medium etc to achieve the mentioned objectives.

On paper the constitution and objectives of HYV are multi-faceted. A glance through the media coverage[48] around, HYV gives some insight on what all they were able to execute. Media has widely covered their activities, events and campaigns around advocacy for Hindu rights, for organizing large scale dinners with people from all castes, organizational meetings, campaigns against social evils like alcoholism, drives against illegal animal movement, *gheraos* of administrative officers to help the poor and needy, drives to help people to get their Aadhar and voter identity cards to avail government benefits and various

48 http://www.hinduyuvavahini.in/samachar.aspx

campaigns against corrupt local and central governments of yester years. Yogi Adityanath led all these interventions directly from the front.

Indian National Congress has designed and promoted the politics of blatant Muslim appeasement over years to secure electoral victories. Regional caste-based parties in Uttar Pradesh also found this formula easy and latched on to it. On one hand, Mulayam Singh mastered the MY (Muslim plus Yadav) combination and on the other hand Mayawati worked for Dalit-Muslim combination to secure Chief Minister's chair. Similar appeasements happened all over the country. Congress at the center and regional satraps in the states have trained and aligned media to suit their narrative. When the rising political star of eastern Uttar Pradesh and someone as strong willed as Yogi Adityanath formed Hindu Yuva Vahini, to protect Hindu rights and work on other social issues, popular media, and left-liberal lobby could not digest it. They started crafting stories to paint HYV communal and started assigning venomous vocabulary to HYV to declare it anti-minority. By the way, a considerable portion of Modi's success can be assigned to false and venomous media attacks on him after unfortunate Godhra incident. With every negative story that was planted, HYV's and Yogi's graph sore.

The likes of Dhirendra K. Jha were not able to digest the rise of Yogi and HYV and wrote a completely biased book on it named, "Yogi Adityanath and the Hindu Yuva Vahini". Jha says in his book that from the moment of its formation, the HYV was steadily embroiled in communal violence. The HYV ran an aggressively toxic campaign, turning even small events into full-blown communal wars and projecting minorities as the enemies of Hindus. Jha went on to add that on the ground the members of the HYV behave nothing less than goons, who obey no one other than their leader. They fondly refer to Adityanath as "Gau Raksha Peethadishwar Parampujya Yogi Adityanath Ji Maharaj" and put on a saffron stole around their necks to distinguish themselves from others. On their website, the group describes themselves as "A fierce cultural and social organization dedicated to

Hindutva and nationalism". To my understanding, Jha never even bothered to look at the charter, constitution and objectives of the organization and largely based his research on some sensational tabloid reporting and his personal hate for saffron color and Hindu philosophy.

Perturbed by the rise of Yogi Adityanath as Chief Minister of Uttar Pradesh, Indian Express[49] (IE) reported recently that while communal riots became a regular feature in Gorakhpur and adjoining areas ever since the inception of the HYV, what is remarkable is the complete silence of the local administration on the activities of the organization. This is unfortunate that in the spree of biased reporting the Indian Express editorial desk completely missed the fact that the numbers of incidents of communal violence had in fact reduced in Gorakhpur and eastern part of Uttar Pradesh, since the rise of Yogi. Also IE's comment of 'silence of local administration, on the activities of the HYV' creates serious doubt on the political acumen of the IE's team as Yogi and HYV largely flourished during BSP and SP governments in UP and Congress lead UPA government in the center.

Observing Yogi and HYV running a purist nationalist agenda, which is completely in line with RSS and BJP, left liberals around the globe seemed very uncomfortable. All of them attempted to document some imaginary rift between the RSS/BJP and the HVY. Political scientist Christophe Jaffrelot[50] tried to force his opinion that HYV's militant Hinduism belongs to a school of thought that widely differs from the BJP's political process. The roots of HYV's political thought, says Jaffrelot, can be traced to Adityanath's predecessor Digvijaynath, who was also the Mahant of the Gorakhnath temple of Gorakhpur. Dhirendra K. Jha, says in his book[51] "Adityanath uses the BJP symbol every time he goes to polls, and yet strives to retain complete hegemony within his fiefdom in eastern Uttar Pradesh, through the

49 What is Yogi Adityanath's Hindu YuvaVahini? http://indianexpress.com/article/what-is/what-is-yogi-adityanaths-hindu-yuva-vahini/

50 http://indianexpress.com/profile/columnist/christophe-jaffrelot/

51 Dhirendra K. Jha, Yogi Adityanath and the Hindu YuvaVahini

Hindu Yuva Vahini (HYV), independent of the RSS and any of its outfits."

Dhirendra K. Jha went one step ahead in his recent article[52] in Scroll.in, where he has crafted a conspiracy theory that RSS asked Adityanath to disband the Hindu Yuva Vahini and all sources of this story are some unknown imaginary insiders. The article says that according to 'BJP insiders', during the state executive meeting of the Bharatiya Janata Party early this month, Keshav Prasad Maurya, Deputy Chief Minister and the president of the BJP's Uttar Pradesh unit, indirectly lashed out at the Hindu Yuva Vahini, saying that 'outsiders' were getting 'preferential treatment' in the government at the cost of party cadres. The article further added that Maurya's outburst came on the concluding day of the meeting, in the presence of Adityanath and Amit Shah, and is believed to have the sanction of the state RSS. Mr. Jha claimed that a member of the party's state executive, who was present at the meeting told him that though Maurya did not take the name of Hindu Yuva Vahini, it was clear to all that he meant this very organization when he referred to outsiders. During my research for the book, all these claims found no ground.

Claims by the likes of Dhirendra K. Jha got some support when it was heard that HYV has indefinitely suspended taking any new memberships[53]. But explaining this, PK Mal, General Secretary of HYV said[54],"In the past, only around 500 to 1,000 people used to contact HYV for membership in a month. But after March 19, since Mahantji (Yogi Adityanath) was sworn in as CM, we are receiving membership requests, including over phone, from more than 5,000 people every day". Mr. Mal further added the erstwhile Samajwadi Party

52 https://scroll.in/article/837614/rss-asks-adityanath-to-disband-the-hindu-yuva-vahini

53 http://economictimes.indiatimes.com/articleshow/58249752.cms?utm_source=contentofinterest&utm_medium=text&utm_campaign=cppst

54 http://www.financialexpress.com/india-news/demand-for-yogi-adityanaths-hindu-yuva-vahini-membership-soars-from-barely-500-per-day-to-5000-after-bjp-leader-becomes-up-cm/612862/

government had sheltered rowdy elements which had run riot in the state and such elements would like to flourish in the present dispensation too by posing as Yuva Vahini members or by becoming members. Hence, they have to be extra careful while inducting any new members and that's why they have stopped the new membership registrations for time being. Anyone posing as HYV member and doing unlawful acts will be sternly punished. Mal added that their existing members should become a *sahyogi* (accomplice) of the local administration in taking government's good work to the masses and work in coordination with the government.

Love Jihad

Yogi Adityanath and his cultural outfit Hindu Yuva Vahini are also accused of spreading concepts like 'Love Jihad' to harass Muslim men and to create anti-minority feeling. Without understanding the whole concept and the underlying social dynamics journalists are busy reporting that nothing of sorts of 'Love Jihad' exists and it's just a figment of imagination of the likes of Yogi Adityanath. Indian Express reported[55] that lately, on the grounds of Love Jihad, HYV has been posing to thwart harassment of women, but in reality became a militant check on Muslim men in relationships with Hindu women, to target the Muslim community.

I conducted a detailed research on the topic, before presenting any verdict to my readers. In his famous article, of 2009, 'The LOVE JIHAD" in the Front Page Mag[56], Stephen Brown said that to the 'hard jihad' of Muslim terrorism and the non-violent, 'stealth jihad', challenging the western societies, the oxymoron 'love jihad' can now be added. But this latest form of Islamist aggression has nothing to do with love.The love jihad's modus operandi involves a heartless strategy of luring vulnerable girls and young

---

55 http://indianexpress.com/article/what-is/what-is-yogi-adityanaths-hindu-yuva-vahini/

56 http://www.frontpagemag.com/fpm/29632/love-jihad-stephen-brown-stephen-brown

women to convert to Islam by feigned love and promises of marriage. But instead of marital bliss, the girls unwittingly get trapped in the deceitful web of Muslim fundamentalist organizations.

When Rajat Sharma of India TV asked Yogi Adityanath, on his famous TV show 'AAP ki Adalat[57]' (Your Court), about Love Jihad, Yogi replied that ex-Chief Minister of Kerala, Shri VS Achuthanandan of CPI(M) was one of the first ones, to express the horrors of Love Jihad. In July 2010[58], describing, 'Love Jihad' Kerala Chief Minister VS Achuthanandan referenced the alleged matrimonial conversion of non-Muslim girls as part of an effort to make Kerala a Muslim majority state.

Allegations of Love Jihad first rose to national awareness in September 2009. Love Jihad was initially alleged to be conducted in Kerala and Mangalore in the coastal Karnataka region. According to the Kerala Catholic Bishops Council (KCBC), by October 2009 up to 4,500 girls in Kerala had been targeted[59], whereas Hindu Janajagruti Samiti claimed that 30,000 girls had been converted in Karnataka alone[60]. Sree Narayana Dharma Paripalana's (SNDP)[61] General Secretary Vellapally Natesan said that there had been reports in Narayaneeya communities of 'Love Jihad' attempts. Reports of similar activities also emerged from Pakistan[62] and the United Kingdom[63]. According to an opinion piece by Liberal

---

57 Yogi Adityanath in Aap Ki Adalat. (2014) https://www.youtube.com/watch?v=WsdqhzaH7qU&t=2390s

58 "Kerala CM criticised for speaking out against 'love jihad'". *The Economic Times*. 27 July 2010. http://economictimes.indiatimes.com/news/politics-and-nation/kerala-cm-criticised-for-speaking-out-against-love-jihad/articleshow/6221406.cms?intenttarget=no

59 http://news.rediff.com/report/2009/oct/14/is-love-jihad-terrors-new-mantra.htm

60 http://www.daijiworld.com/news/newsDisplay.aspx?newsID=66952

61 http://www.newindianexpress.com/states/kerala/2009/oct/19/sndp-to-join-fight-against-love-jihad-95789.html

62 http://timesofindia.indiatimes.com/world/pakistan/Not-just-White-girls-Pak-Muslim-men-sexually-target-Hindu-and-Sikh-girls-as-well/articleshow/7254035.cms?referral=PM

63 http://www.standard.co.uk/news/police-protect-girls-forced-to-convert-to-islam-7256407.html

Politics blogger[64] Sunny Hundal, "In the 90s, an anonymous leaflet (suspected to be by Hizbut-Tahrir followers) urged Muslim men to seduce Sikh girls to convert them to Islam in Britain". In 2014[65], national Taekwondo player from UP said she was a love jihad victim.

Over years, many leaders in political and social spheres raised the issue of Love Jihad. In December 2011, in Karnataka Legislative Assembly, Mallika Prasad of the Bhartiya Janata Party asserted[66] that the problem of Love Jihad is ongoing and unaddressed. According to her, 69 of 84 Hindu girls who had gone missing in Karnataka confessed, after their recovery, that they'd been lured by Muslim youths who professed love. On 25 June 2012, Oommen Chandy, then Chief Minister of Kerala, tabled some numbers around love Jihad in the state Legislature[67]. Chandy told the house that, 7,713 people converted to Islam between 2006 and 2012 2,195 Hindu women converted to Islam between 2009 and 2012 and 492 Christian women converted to Islam during 2009-2012. In September 2014, BJP MP Sakshi Maharaj claimed that Muslim boys in madrasas are being motivated for Love Jihad with proposals of rewards of, Rs 11 lakh for an 'affair' with a Sikh girl, Rs 10 lakh for a Hindu girl and Rs 7 lakh for a Jain girl. Yogi Adityanath in his interview with Rajat Sharma told that Muslim boys lure *Hindu* girls with disguised names and they have award packages for these love jihad missions.

Courts also recognized the phenomenon of Love Jihad and commented against it in various cases. On 9 December 2009, Justice K T Sankaran[68]of the Kerala High Court, suspected a clear love jihad angle, during a bail hearing for a Muslim

---

64 https://www.theguardian.com/commentisfree/belief/2012/jul/03/edl-sikh-men-women

65 http://indiatoday.intoday.in/story/love-jihad-taekwondo-national-player-from-kanpur-up/1/380151.html

66 http://timesofindia.indiatimes.com/city/bangalore/Love-jihad-sparks-hate/articleshow/11140332.cms?referral=PM

67 http://www.firstpost.com/india/keralas-missing-youths-spate-of-conversions-love-jihad-cases-hint-at-more-disappearances-2890416.html

68 http://articles.economictimes.indiatimes.com/2009-12-10/news/28410696_1_love-jihad-religious-conversions-religions

youth arrested for allegedly forcibly converting two campus girls. According to Sankaran, police reports revealed the 'blessings of some outfits' for a 'concerted' effort for religious conversions. Some 3,000 to 4,000 conversion incidences had taken place after love affairs in a four year period. Sankaran found indications of 'forceful' religious conversions under the garb of 'love', suggesting that such 'deceptive' acts might require legislative intervention to prevent them.

In 2017, CBI filed a charge sheet in an alleged case of 'Love Jihad' involving national-level shooter Tara Shahdeo. It was filed against Ranjeet Singh Kohli, who she had alleged had forced her to convert to marry him. The charge sheet was filed in Ranchi court under sections of criminal conspiracy, sexual assault, domestic violence and fraudulently organizing a marriage ceremony without a lawful wedding. After the marriage, Shahdeo, found that Kohli's real name was Raqibul Hasan Khan. She told the police and the CBI that she was tortured for over a month to accept her husband's religion, reported Subhajit Sengupta of News18[69].

Yogi Adityanath raised the issues of Love Jihad in his region and fought hard against it. Oblivious of all these facts, popular media has been busy denying the issue of love jihad completely.

2005, Mass Re-conversion (Ghar Wapsi)

In October 2005, Adityanath led a 'purification drive' in the district of Etah, in Uttar Pradesh, converting 1,800 Christians to Hinduism. Earlier that year, he had converted 5,000 Dalit Christians in the same district[70].

When asked by Rajat Sharma of IndiaTv on his TV show 'Aapki Adalat' about this mass conversion incident, Yogi accepted the allegation with great pride and said, that these were people who were forced to leave their Hindu faith due

69 http://www.news18.com/news/india/a-first-cbi-chargesheet-in-an-alleged-case-of-love-jihad-1409143.html

70 http://www.newindianexpress.com/nation/2017/mar/18/what-does-yogi-adityanath-stand-for-here-are-five-statements-of-his-that-reflect-who-he-is-1582926.html

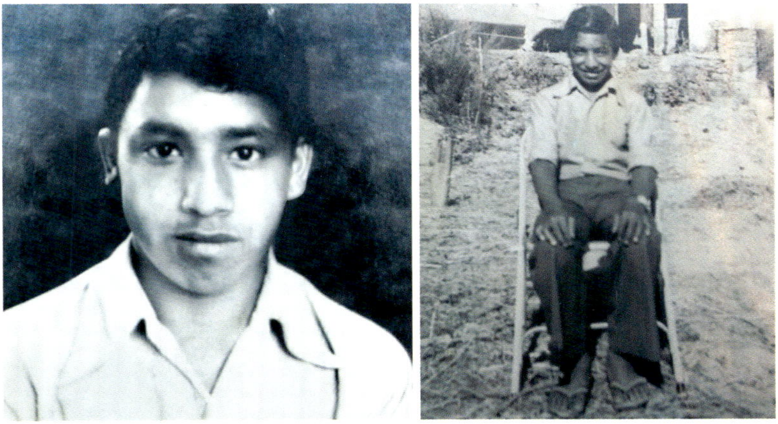

Ajay Singh Bisht, while growing up in Panchur Village, Uttarakhand

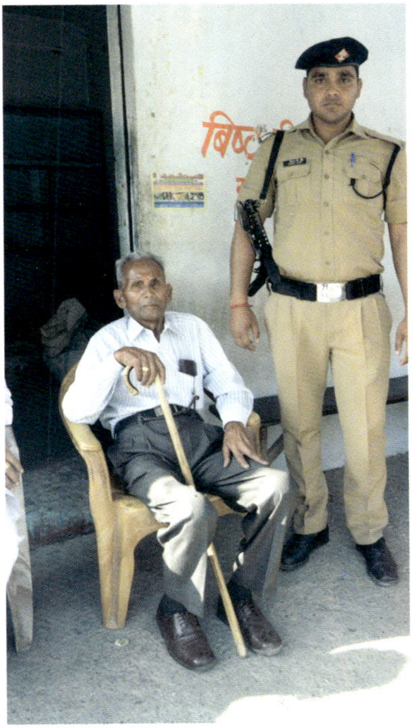

Anand Singh Bisht,
Yogi Adityanath's father

Savita Devi,
Yogi Adityanath's mother

House at Panchur (Uttarakhand), where Ajay grew

Bharat Mandir Intercollege, Rishikesh, where Ajay did his 11th and 12th grade

Ajay's teachers Shri Bansi Dhar Pokhriyal and Shri DPS Rawat, at Bharat Mandir Intercollege, Rishikesh, showing Ajay's seat

PG College, Kotdwar (Uttarakhand), where Ajay did his graduation

Pandit Lalit Mohan Sharma Government PG College, Rishikesh (Uttarakhand), where Ajay enrolled for MSc, first year

Ajay with friends, during college days, sporting a bandana

Ajay with friends, during college days, sporting goggles

Gorakhnath Mutt (aka Gorakshanath Mandir)

Guru Matsyendranath's statue at Gorakhnath Mutt

Guru Gorakshnath's statue at Gorakhnath Mutt

Ajay's diksha (initiation) as a Nath Panth Sanyasi. Making of Yogi Adityanath

Mahant Avaidyanath speaking, during diksha of Yogi Adityanath

VHP's Ashok Singhal ji speaking, during diksha of Yogi Adityanath

Yogi Adityanath helping flood victims

Yogi Adityanath performing pooja

A Kanphata sadhu at Gorakhdham Mutt, with clay earring

Yogi Adityanath washing a girl child's feet

Yogi Adityanath spending time with children

Yogi Adityanath staging a protest under the Hindu Yuva Vahini banner

Yogi Adityanath listening to the problems of people at the *Janta Darbar* in Gorakhpur

Yogi Adityanath listening to the problems of people, at CM House, after becoming Chief Minister

Yogi Adityanath, addressing a large gathering

Yogi Adityanath, feeding milk to a lion cub

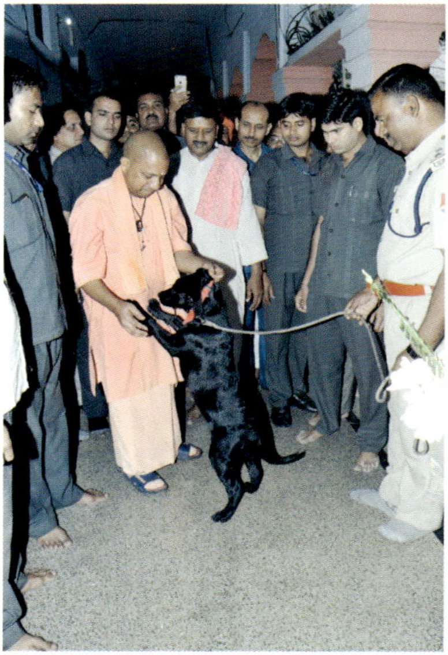

Yogi Adityanath, playing with his dog

Yogi Adityanath is fond of nature and animals

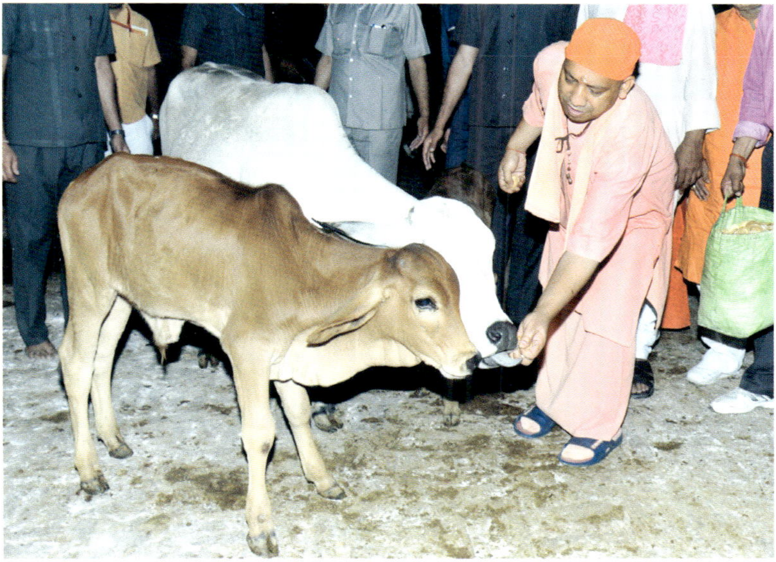

Yogi Adityanath, feeding jaggery to the cows at Gaushala

Cremation ceremony of Mahant Avaidyanath

Yogi Adityanath's anointment as Mahant of Gorakhnath Mutt

Yogi Adityanath visiting the Indian National Army Monument in Singapore

Yogi Adityanath on a foreign tour with close associate Arunesh Shahi

PM Narendra Modi's visit to Gorakhnath Mutt

PM Narendra Modi and others discussing the AIIMS, Gorakhpur's prototype

Yogi Adityanath ji with Shri Ashok Singhal of Vishwa Hindu Parishad (VHP)

Shri Mohan Bhagwat, Sarsanghchalak of Rashtriya Swayamsevak Sangh (RSS) visiting Gorakhnath Mutt. Yogi's close associates Dwarka Prasad Tiwari and Pradeep Rao can be seen (*right*)

Yogi Adityanath with senior party leader LK Advani

Yogi Adityanath with Shri Amit Shah, national president of the Bhartiya Janta Party (BJP)

Yogi Adityanath taking oath as the 21st Chief Minister of Uttar Pradesh

Yogi Adityanath meeting PM Narendra Modi after taking oath as the Chief Minister of Uttar Pradesh

Yogi Adityanath practising yoga with Baba Ramdev

Yogi Adityanath, with close associate Rajbhushan Singh Rawat (*right*) at 5 Kalidas Marg, Lucknow

Yogi Adityanath, at CM residence in Lucknow, with BJP, UP organisational secretary, Shri Sunil Bansal

Yogi Adityanath is very active on Facebook and posted his meeting with President Shri Ram Nath Kovind

Yogi Adityanath is active on Twitter (now X) and posted his meeting with Sadguru Jaggi Vasudev

to fear, temptation and coercion and they are now retuning home (*Ghar Vapsi*) to their original faith.

Article 25 of the Indian Constitution guarantees freedom to practice religion in India. In the garb of freedom of religion, missionary groups execute massive conversion drives, mainly in poor pockets of India through coercion and temptation. Several Indian states passed Freedom of Religion bills primarily to prevent people from converting to Christianity. Odisha was the first state to bring such a law called 'Orissa Freedom of Religion Act, 1967[71]. It was followed by Madhya Pradesh in 1968 and Arunachal Pradesh in 1978. Catholics protested against this saying that propagation of their faith was an important part of Christianity. Both laws enacted by the Odisha and Madhya Pradesh High Courts were challenged stating Article 25 of the Constitution. The Supreme Court supported the State, saying, "What is freedom for one is freedom for the other in equal measure and there can, therefore, be no such thing as a fundamental right to convert any person to one's own religion".

Later many other states adopted anti-conversion laws that prohibit forced conversions or conversions induced through money. Chhattisgarh in 2000 and Gujarat State in 2003 also passed anti-conversion laws. In July 2006, the Madhya Pradesh government passed legislation requiring people, who desire to convert to a different religion to provide the government with one month's notice, or face fines and penalties. In August 2006, the Chhattisgarh State Assembly passed similar legislation requiring anyone who desires to convert to another religion to give 30 days' notice to, and seek permission from, the district magistrate. In February 2007, Himachal Pradesh became the first Congress Party-ruled state to adopt legislation banning illegal religious conversions. Rajasthan followed it in 2008.

71 http://www.thehindu.com/thehindu/op/2002/12/17/stories/2002121700110200.htm

With Yogi Adityanath, a known crusader against forced conversions, at the helm of affairs in Uttar Pradesh, we may see such an anti-conversion law in Uttar Pradesh soon.

2007, Arrest of Yogi Adityanath

In January 2007, a few Muslims groups went unruly during a Muharram procession in Gorakhpur and started teasing some Hindu girls. When a young Hindu boy, Raj Kumar Agrahari protested, he was brutally beaten by the Muslim men and Raj Kumar Agrahari was hospitalized. Under pressure from the Mulayam Singh government, district administration took no serious action against the criminals. Instead the District Magistrate advised Yogi Adityanath not to visit the incident site as it could create tensions. Adityanath initially agreed, but after Agrahari died, Yogi was not able to control himself and he disobeyed the magistrate and travelled to the site and started a non-violent *dharna* on the site with a group of followers. As Yogi was exposing the lack of action by the local administration due to the Muslim appeasement policies of Mulayam government, local police declared a curfew, to create a trap for Yogi's arrest as they knew Yogi would not sit silent and would certainly be with the people. As expected, Adityanath broke the curfew and he was subsequently arrested and remanded for a fortnight on charges of 'disturbing peace', while no concrete action was taken against the murderers of Raj Kumar Agrahari, said Pradeep Rao, a close aide of Yogi Adityanath. Rao also added that nothing more could have been expected from a JNU alum, Hari Om, who was the District Magistrate then. District Magistrate and Police Chief wanted to house-arrest Yogi in the temple premise, but Yogi insisted them to take him to jail. As the Police vehicle with Yogi moved on the streets of Gorakhpur, people laid down in front of the car. Police had to physically move two-three people at one time and then drive the vehicle ahead by a few meters. It took the administration more than 8 hours to cover a distance of two kilometers. That day the world witnessed the popularity of this monk. This extreme attitude of Muslim appeasement by the Mulayam government gave rise to a harsh wave of anger among the local majority population of Gorakhpur and they came out on the streets to protest. As an eyewash the Samajvadi government transferred the District Magistrate and the district police chief.

In the very next budget session in the parliament, Yogi exposed the Mulayam government in front of the whole nation. Addressing the Chair, Yogi said with a very heavy heart and with tears in eyes[72], "Speaker Sir, I have become a Member of the Parliament for the third time from Gorakhpur Lok Sabha seat. The first time I won with 25000 votes, second time with 50000 and the third time with1.5 lakh votes. But for quite some time now I am being targeted because of the political enmity. Sir, I just came here to ask you that whether I am the member of this House or not, and whether this House can give me protection?" Yogi further added, "If this House cannot give me the protection, then I better leave the house and go back. This does not have any importance for me. I have taken *sanyas* (renunciation for worldly life) for the society, I have left my family, my parents, but today I am being called a culprit only because of political bias. All this has happened because I raised the matter of corruption in the State, because I raised my voice against the anti-national activities of ISI along the India-Nepal border and regularly sought attention of the House, I raised the matter of the hunger deaths caused due to the administrative corruption. Sir, this is the reason why so many cases are being built against me".

But Yogi's two decades of tough fight against a heartless and corrupt opposition finally bore fruit. With all the expertise and experience of working for the people, today he heads the state of Uttar Pradesh.

---

72 **Yogi Adityanath Cried in Lok Sabha** www.youtube.com/watch?v=WS96DDrWAzw

2008, Fatal attack on Yogi Adityanath

In August 2007, three weeks after the serial blasts that rocked Ahmedabad, killing 57 people, Gujarat police claimed a major breakthrough with the arrest of 10 activists of the banned Students Islamic Movement of India (SIMI), including 9 from Gujarat. The formal announcement of these arrests was made only after the alleged mastermind, Mufti Abdul Bashar Kasmi, was picked up from Sarai Meer locality in Azamgarh district of Uttar Pradesh. A Gujarat police team struggled to convince their reluctant UP counterparts about Bashar's involvement and it took some phone calls between higher-ups in the two states to sort things out, as reported by Times of India[73].

Following Abdul Bashar's arrest, a public meeting was organized by some local Muslim groups in Azamgarh to show support and solidarity to the SIMI activist. Yogi Adityanath was outraged by government's and administration's silence on this open public support to a terrorist. Mulayam's love for SIMI was known, but in 2008, it was Mayawati's government in Uttar Pradesh and the level of Muslim appeasement was no less. Local administration kept quiet, but Yogi did not. On 7 September 2008, under Yogi's leadership, Hindu Yuva Vahini along with BJP organized a massive anti-terrorism rally at the DAV ground in Azamgarh to protest the public support for terrorists.

While narrating the incident Pradeep Rao, said that while Yogi was travelling towards the rally location in his cavalcade, his vehicle was 11th in the order, in the longtrail of red color safari cavalcade. He got a tipoff from one of his *karyakartas* (volunteer), about a possible attack on him down the road. On his way to Azamgarh, he stopped over in a government guesthouse for a short while and moved to position three in the cavalcade. When Yogi's cavalcade was passing though Takia area, in Azamgarh, unaware of this change in the vehicle sequence, a Muslim group launched a brutal pre-planned attack on vehicle 10th, 11th and 12th,

73 http://timesofindia.indiatimes.com/india/Ahmedabad-blasts-brains-SIMI-man-techie/articleshow/3370648.cms

thinking Yogi was still in vehicle number 11. They attacked first with sticks, stones and fire torches and then with bullets. As volunteers in these vehicles were also alerted in advance, they moved out in time. Yogi's vehicle escaped this attack and reached the rally ground. He addressed the rally without any hue and cry and without even referring to the attack on his cavalcade. In his speech, he said that all elements that are supporting terrorists should be dealt strictly and petty politics should not be played in the matters of national security. He also said that those organizing meetings and protesting arrest of terrorists and their agents are anti-nationals, who should be brought to book, as reported by Hindustan Times[74].

In spite of Yogi not speaking about it, the news of the attack on him became big by the evening. BJP came in support of it's MP and condemned the attack and demanded an enquiry into the incident. Senior BJP leader and then party General Secretary, Arun Jaitley said, "We condemn the attack on Yogi Adityanath's convoy in Azamgarh. This attack appears to have been inspired by those who are aggrieved with the arrest of terrorists who were allegedly involved in Ahmedabad blasts. We demand a thorough enquiry and action against the guilty[75]."

A few days later on September 12, Mayawati Government suspended Azamgarh DIG Abhimanyu Tripathi and SP V K Garg as an eyewash, as reported by News Nation[76]. In a recent interview with India TV, Yogi narrated this incident and commented that administration knew about the plan of the attack on him much in advance, but did not take any action[77].

---

74 http://www.hindustantimes.com/india/one-killed-six-injured-in-attack-on-bjp-mp-s-convoy/story-wHvBHKlkmTaiege2zgnnpO.html

75 http://zeenews.india.com/home/bjp-mp-yogi-adityanaths-convoy-attacked-7-injured_467356.html

76 http://www.newsnation.in/india-news/when-yogi-adityanath-motorcade-was-attacked-by-a-mob-in-azamgarh-in-2008-video-article-165044.html

77 https://www.youtube.com/watch?v=xshgEQfGca4&t=4043s

Since Yogi Adityanath has become the Chief Minister of Uttar Pradesh, popular media, has covered at length his various speeches. They have covered instances of when he cried in the Parliament, of how he formed Hindu Yuva Vahini, why was he jailed by Mulayam government and they even covered his shaving schedule. Surprisingly the media did not find enough airtime to talk much about the fatal attack on Yogi by Muslim groups in Azamgarh. The habit of Muslim appeasement has been injected so deep in the society during the long Congress lead dispensation that its hangover is still continuing.

Yogi's Controversial Speeches and Statements

Yogi comes across as a man on a mission. He sounds angry in his speeches. When I enquired about Yogi as a person, his close aides said that by the time Yogi became socially and politically active, he realized that Congress party and the strong regional parties had converted politics into mere electoral mathematics. The formula invented by these parties to master the electoral mathematics in Uttar Pradesh and many other parts of the country is to blindly appease Muslims and to keep Hindus divided by castes. Yogi determined to break this nexus and over years his anger on blatant Muslim appeasement has been seen through his speeches.

Those who oppose Surya Namaskar can leave India

He is not someone who minces word. While commenting on the opposition on Surya Namaskar, a famous yogic exercise by some Muslim groups, he came out full throttle saying that those who oppose Surya Namaskar can leave India. He also made a request that those who see communalism in even Sun God should drown themselves in the sea or live in a dark room for the rest of their lives, reported by The Hindu[78].

---

78 http://www.thehindu.com/news/national/other-states/yogi-adityanath-says-those-who-avoid-yoga-can-leave-india/article7297946.ece

If they take one Hindu girl, we will take 100 Muslims girls

In an undated video that surfaced on YouTube during August 2014, Adityanath, reportedly during a public speech at Azamgarh, referring to the religious conversions due to inter-religious marriages, was seen saying, "If they take one Hindu girl, we will take 100 Muslims girls." In the same video, he continued to say, "If they kill one Hindu, there will be 100 that we" and paused, as the gathered crowd shouted, "Kill", reported by The Hindustan Times.[79]

In an interview with Rajat Sharma of IndiaTV, Yogi explained his point further, that a yogi (saint) is trained to use both – a *mala* (beads) and a *bhaala* (spear). A yogi knows both – *shaastras* (religious text) and *shastra* (weapons) and for a peaceful living, a yogi has to use both. He said that silence should not be taken as weakness. When asked, how he can take law in his own hands, Yogi replied, "they (Muslim) keep attacking our people, our daughters and the local administration keep mum, we have to fight out our own battle."

If given a chance, we will install statues of Goddess Gauri, Ganesh and Nandi in every mosque

It is well documented that, Mughals and other Muslim invaders have destroyed many Hindu temples, monuments, universities and burnt ancient Vedic literature over the years. This issue is close to Yogi's heart. Yogi was speaking at the Vishwa Hindu Parishad's 'Virat Hindu Sammelan' organized as part of its golden jubilee year celebration in Varanasi. While referring to the Gyan-vapi mosque which was built by Mughal Emperor Aurangzeb after he demolished the original Kashi Vishwanath temple, Yogi said, "Has it happened anywhere in the world that Gauri and Ganesh are placed inside a mosque? Every time a Hindu visits the Vishwanath temple, the Gyan-vapi mosque taunts us. If given a chance, we will install statues of Goddess Gauri,

79 http://www.hindustantimes.com/assembly-elections/from-love-jihad-conversion-to-srk-10-controversial-comments-by-up-s-new-cm-yogi-adityanath/story-5JW2ZFGZzAdIZeIcjcZCNM.html

Ganesh and Nandi in every mosque", reported Amita Verma of Deccan Chronicle.[80]

Yogi further said, "Everyone, irrespective of religion, can come to Kashi, but only Muslims are allowed in Mecca and Medina. This is the century of Hindutva, not just in India, but in the entire world."

SRK talks like Hafiz Saeed, can go to Pakistan

During the intolerance debate in the Indian media in late 2015, Adityanath commented that actor Shah Rukh Khan was using the same 'language' as Pakistani terrorist Hafiz Saeed. He had said, "Shah Rukh Khan should remember that majority population of the country made him the star, and if they boycott his films, he will also have to wander on streets", reported Indian Express.[81]

Mother Teresa was part of a conspiracy for 'Christianisation' of India

As reported by Manomohan Rai of ET[82], Speaking at a religious meeting in Basti in June, 2016, Yogi Adityanath said: "Mother Teresa was part of a conspiracy to convert Hindus to Christianity. Hindus were targeted in the name of doing service and then converted by her." Large-scale conversions to Christianity in the Northeast had led to a separatist movement in Arunachal Pradesh, Tripura, Meghalaya and Nagaland, he said. "You are in a majority here so you do not know the conditions that Hindus face in NE. You should go and see the situation to realize what is happening," he said.

---

80 http://www.deccanchronicle.com/150210/nation-current-affairs/article/given-chance-will-put-ganesh-idols-all-mosques-yogi-adityanath

81 http://indianexpress.com/article/india/india-news-india/no-difference-between-shah-rukh-khan-and-hafiz-saeed-yogi-adityanath/#sthash.Mgfk4X9E.dpuf

82 http://economictimes.indiatimes.com/news/politics-and-nation/bjp-mp-yogi-adityanath-accuses-mother-teresa-of-religious-conversion/articleshow/52842431.cms

Bharatiya Janata Party (BJP) leader Subramanian Swamy on extended support to his party MP Yogi Adityanath, who accused Mother Teresa of being part of a 'conspiracy to Christianise India', saying the views are not isolated, as there have been books published in this regard.

ANI reported[83] that, Swamy said, "You see the issue of Yogi Adityanath expressing his view is not an isolated view. It is a view which has been reduced to books, there is a writer Christopher Hitchens, who has written a best seller book and if you go to Google you would get a lots of books about her,"

Citing an example, Swamy said once a prominent crook, who robbed the pensions of middle class people in California was caught and a trial was taking place and Mother Teresa wrote a letter asking not to prosecute him, as he has given her millions of dollars to further the cause of Christianity in India. "The judge responded that he was surprised that Mother Teresa was coming on his behalf, as he has robbed the pension of hard working people and in the name of Jesus Christ, asked him to return the money, so that relief can be given to the people," Swamy said.

Taj mahal does not reflect Indian culture

Uttar Pradesh Chief Minister Yogi Adityanath, who does not believe in too much political correctness when speaking his mind, got himself into another controversy when he suggested that the Taj Mahal and other such monuments "did not reflect Indian culture.", as reported by R Jagannathan of Swarajya[84]. Foreign dignitaries, he said, were now being given copies of the Gita and the Ramayana where earlier they were being given replicas of the Taj[85]. There is an intrinsic truth to what Yogi was trying to convey.

83 http://www.business-standard.com/article/politics/subramanian-swamy-backs-yogi-adityanath-s-attack-on-mother-teresa-116062200192_1.html

84 https://swarajyamag.com/ideas/politically-incorrect-it-may-be-but-there-is-an-underlying-truth-to-yogi-adityanaths-views-on-taj-mahal

85 https://www.youtube.com/watch?v=gQdbR52FeXo

The true spirit of India is not defined by the monuments to human vanity that were left behind by past rulers, but the civilizational ethos, culture and spiritual pursuits of its people, wrote R Jagannathan.

Satan could change for the better, but Pakistan cannot

On 3 January 2016, a day after the terrorist attack on an Indian air force base in Pathankot allegedly by Pakistani terrorists, Adityanath compared Pakistan to Satan. Adityanath blamed the assault on Pakistan, claiming, "The Pathankot attack has once again proved that Satan could change for the better, but Pakistan cannot", reported The Tribune.[86]

Praised Trump's travel ban for some Muslims countries

Adityanath has praised the US President Donald Trump's decision to enact a ban on citizens from 7 Muslim-majority countries entering the United States and has called for India to adopt similar policies to tackle terrorism, reported NDTV.[87]

Yogi's defense on his so-called controversial speeches

Speaking in the Parliament, on 13 August, 2014, during the debate on communal violence in India, Yogi made an eloquent speech, giving a detailed account of the blatant Muslim appeasement by Congress and other regional parties over the years, which led to wide spread anger among the majority Hindu community. This meticulous speech will give my readers an insight into Yogi's anger that is reflected in all his hard-hitting speeches.

Yogi said on the floor of the Parliament[88], "I was surprised that when he (referring to Congress leader Mallikarjun Kharge) was reading his statement here, he said that 113 incidents happened, but when he was speaking, he said

---

86 https://tribune.com.pk/story/1021226/this-bjp-mp-thinks-pakistan-is-worse-than-satan/

87 http://www.ndtv.com/india-news/bjps-yogi-adityanath-praises-donald-trumps-immigration-ban-says-india-needs-it-1654430

88 https://www.youtube.com/watch?v=kNuJRmMHYTg

that more than 600 incidents happened. What is the truth? I guess the whole country knows. On 26 May, 2014, under the guidance of Shri Narendra Modi, BJP government has taken oath and after the new government trust resumed among people towards governance and administration after a long time. I will take you through the data that was given by the Honorable Mr. Kharge. If Mr. Kharge believes in his data, if he accepts his data and if they are really serious about the communal violence in the country then they need to apologize to the people of this country for the numerous policy declarations made by them on the communal basis.

Speaker Sir, I am talking about 2011, when neither at the center not at the states that I am referring to had a BJP government. As per 2011 report, 580 incidents of communal violence happened in the country, where 91 people died and 1899 were injured of which the maximum number of incidents about 84 happened in Uttar Pradesh, where 12 people were died and 347 were injured. On the second position was Maharashtra, where 88 incidents happened in which 15 died and it was Congress government ruling the state at the time. On the third position was Karnataka with 70 incidents and there also it was a Congress government. After that it was Kerala where 30 incidents happened.

In 2012, 668 incidents happened in which 94 died and 2117 were injured. In 2013 it was Congress government at the center and 823 incidents of communal violence occurred in the entire nation. Law and order is a state subject and local police administration behaves according to the will and leadership of the state government. If they (Congress) had introspected honestly about their own and their allies' agenda, they would have understood why this polarization is happening? What are the reasons of polarization? If we talk about polarization, on one hand they (Congress) say that they are secular, but on the other hand the agenda that they implement is totally communal.

In this country more than 12 lakhs saints and priests live, but these people (Congress and their allies) declare salaries only for *'Imaams'* (Muslim priests). They only declare one-sided policies. Is this is a secular agenda? Same was done by the government of Delhi, by the government of West Bengal and also by the government of Maharashtra, during non-BJP governments. Is this their secular agenda? They divide the society on the communal basis and, Speaker Sir, on the same lines I will talk about Uttar Pradesh. Schemes in Uttar Pradesh have 20 per cent reservation for Muslims. For the boundary walls of graveyards (Muslim burial grounds), disputes were created in every village to grab land. Samajvadi government allocated 300 crores for the same. Supreme Court has already said that there should be no land grabbing of any public property in the name of temple, mosque, and other religious pretexts. But in Uttar Pradesh the illegal land grabbing is going on unstopped in the name of the graveyards. All this is going unchecked as government promotes it and so the local administration remains silent. If this is the case, will the communal polarization not happen?

Likewise, the situation gets even worse when cases filed against terrorists are taken back. These are criminals, who are dangerous to the national security; people who are regularly challenging the sovereignty of India, and inflicting violence. Cases against such terrorists are being taken back! This includes culprits of Ram '*Janm Bhoomi*' attack, culprits of the CRPF camp attack at Sankat Mochan Temple in Kashi and the culprits of the serial blasts in Gorakhpur. In all these cases, Uttar Pradesh Government has tried their best to take back the cases against these terrorists just for the sake of their vote bank. Thank God that we have courts in this country; otherwise those terrorists would have been out there and could have killed people on the streets of the country.

Speaker Sir, the topic of debate should be that who is actually communal? And I think it is necessary to debate on this topic. Sir, as I know, someone who says that only his or her almighty is great is communal. His followers have right to live, but not the rest. I think that is communal. Our message is '*Krinvanto Vishwam Aryam*' (To Make the World Noble), we have given the message of '*Sarvé Bhavantu*

Sukhinaḥ' (May All become Happy) and we have talked about *'Ekam Sat Vipra Bahudha Vadanti'* (Truth is one, but the learned refer to it in different names). Our ideology is live and let others live, and there is no religion in this world that Hinduism hasn't given protection to and the opportunities to grow in their difficult times. But today it is unfortunate that strategies are made against Hinduism, a religion that has given protection to others for centuries. We, the Hindus need to stand in unity to challenge it and it is because of such people that today, the Hindus of this country think that they need to stand in unity to retaliate against the conspiracies and strategies crafted against them. Sir, I would like to tell the House that when a Muslim from Indian sub-continent goes for 'Haj' his identity is not made in the name of India, Pakistan, or Bangladesh, but it is made in the name 'Hindu'. But they feel bad about 'Hindu' identity back in India. Hindu is the symbol of nationality not religion or community and if someone defames the symbol of nationality of India then he or she will have to pay the price for it.

Sir through you, I would like to inform the house that Gurudev Rabindranath Tagore once said if you want to understand India, first you should know about Indian culture and to understand Indian culture, first you should know about Swami Vivekananda. Swami Vivekananda preached, 'Say with Pride, that we are Hindus'. Swami Vivekananda wasn't communal. He wasn't from any party. He represented India throughout the world. The Hindus who are known for their tolerance throughout the world, are facing such a behavior.

In the year 2012 in Assam, people of Bodo caste were killed, but nobody spoke on their behalf in the house. Opposition never spoke a word, here in the House, in support of 3.5 lacs of Kashmiri Pandits, who were thrown out of Kashmir. This is one of the biggest examples when people are living the life of a nomad within their own country. Opposition never condemned such a shameful act. They (opposition) were silent on the Mumbai riots. The riots of Jamshedpur and

Bhagalpur happened during the Congress rule. They don't show any remorse for that. They never feel ashamed of the mass murder of the Sikhs in 1984 by Congress leaders and workers. With such a murky record, these people are talking about communal harmony? Their faces are colored with a history of instigating communal violence and designing communal agendas.

What's happening in Assam today? Intruders from Bangladesh have become their own and communities that have been living there for thousands of years are left feeling like outsiders. In 2011-2012, rioting continued in Assam for almost three months, but not a single debate was organized about it in the house. In fact once they singled out their own Chief Minister for Assam for speaking in favor of Bodo people. Intruders from Bangladesh seem dearer to them and they are advocating only for them. Speaker Sir, intruders from Bangladesh have changed the whole demography of the place. Kokrajhar, Dhubri, Chirang and Barpeta districts of Assam, witness the highest number of incidents of violence. These are same districts that have the highest number of intruders from Bangladesh who come in and try to grab lands from locals by violent means. Opposition has played with the national interests of the country; by giving them ration cards and work permits, just to create a vote bank.

I want to ask the members of Congress and Communist parties why they called for a special session of assembly in Kerala to facilitate the release of the dreaded terrorist behind Coimbatore Blast? Both the parties appealed together for his release. Is this their secular agenda? Is this the secularism of this country?

Speaker Sir, we have not forgotten what happened in this country on August 11, 2012, on Azad grounds in Mumbai. A violent protest was organized by local Muslim groups to show solidarity, with Rohingya Muslims of Myanmar, against the violent incident between Rohingya Muslims and Buddhists. It happened in Myanmar and had nothing to do with India. These protesting Muslim groups broke *Shaheed Smarak* at Azad grounds, and attacked police and media personnel.

For this totally un-related incident, Pune witnessed rioting. In Uttar Pradesh, Bareilly, Lucknow, Kanpur, Allahabad witnessed violence. They let it all pass silently. These are the same people *(pointing towards opposition benches in the house)*, who were silent on the unfortunate incidents of Azad ground. They are the ones who cruelly lathi charged the nationalists singing *vande matram*, along with Baba Ramdev at midnight. And now they talk about communal violence in the country? It's apparent now, that who is spreading communal violence in the country and who is attempting to divide the society in the name of Sachar Committee report? They have divided the country on communal grounds in 1947 and now they are attempting the same again and dancing to the tunes of Pakistan.

It is clear that the Opposition has a communal agenda, not us. We have always tried to keep the country together. Our slogan is '*Sabka Sath aur Sabka Vikas*'. But in Assam they gave a dividing slogan of 'Ali' and 'Kuli'. They are conspiring to separate Assam from the country. Is this their secularism?

I want to discuss about Uttar Pradesh. In UP, 118 communal incidents happened in 2012. 247 communal incidents happened in 2013 and up to May 2014, 65 incidents had happened. Why did Saharanpur riots occur? In Saharanpur, one Gurudwara was being built as per High Court's order. But UP government did not care about Court rulings. Why did Kant violence take place? A village of Kant had four religious structures. Three mosques and a temple. All the three Mosques had mikes, but only the Temple's mike was removed forcibly. Is this a secular agenda? Is this their secularism? Be it kidnapping and rape of a young girl in Meerut by a particular community, they are always silent. Balance of justice, will thrive only when justice is same for all. Justice cannot be applied partially on the basis of one's religion. Yogi ended his speech saying that Speaker Sir, through you I want to request the Honorable Home Minister, to get an SIT enquiry done into all these incidents by a sitting judge of the Supreme Court. SIT enquiry should also check who has connections with anti-national elements.

What Muslims have to say about Yogi

Over years, media has painted Yogi as anti-muslim, but the reality is quite different. It is noteworthy that the responsibility of all the construction work in the Gorakhdham Mutt is with Mohd. Yasin Ansari. Talking to ABP TV[89], Mr. Ansari, said, "I have been associated with the temple since 1977. I am responsible for all the construction work here. Be it the temple compound, the meditation room or the tourist residence; all the work is executed by my team. There are absolutely no restrictions for me to go inside the temple."

Dr. Mushtaq who runs his clinic in Gorakhpur told ABP News reporter Pratima Mishra that a wrong image of Yogi Adityanath has been created and that their community is very happy with their Maharaj Ji becoming the Chief Minister. Dr. Mushtaq specially mentioned that in a crowd of 50-100 people, Maharaj ji spots the person with beard or Muslim attire and attends to him or her on priority.

People at the Madarsa Ziaul Uloom, in old Gorakhpur told ABP News reporter, that Yogi Adityanath reacted quickly when Maulana's of the Madarsa reported about the illegal land grabbing by some anti-social elements. Yogi contacted the concerned Police officers and got the case settled within hours.

Many people from the Muslim community have shops inside the Mutt's compound and many others are dependent on the Mutt for their livelihood, directly or indirectly. Even in Uttarakhand, where the Mutt has setup the, Mahayogi Guru Gorakhnath College, near Yogi Adityanath's native village, Dr. Aftab Ahmed, Professor of Economics, is the head of the institution.

Yogi's Relationship with the BJP

Media has forced us to believe that Adityanath has strained relations with the BJP for over a decade. I tried to enquire into

89 https://www.youtube.com/watch?v=hMaSjyjfMyo

this aspect in detail during my research for this biography. I observed that the media is used to the dictatorial Central leadership and the yes-boss culture of the grand old ruling party, the Indian National Congress (INC). Any democratic, decent argument or counter-argument was termed as being rebellious by the popular media.

Yogi Adityanath, being a yogi was always completely aligned to BJP's nationalistic ideology. Being a purist, he advised and warned the party, whenever he felt there was dilution in the nationalist ideology. Over the years, he has established a strong base in the eastern regions of Uttar Pradesh, through regular *Janta Darbars*, by raising the voice of the people from local government offices to the Parliament of the country and through various welfare services delivered by the Gorakhnath Mutt. Being a strong and popular local leader he always had advice for the party for local decisions like fielding candidates in different types of elections. Like any other strong local leader he always pushed for his advice strongly.

The most prominent example being quoted was the fielding of Radha Mohan Das Agarwal, in 2002, from Gorakhpur on a Hindu Mahasabha ticket who eventually defeated BJP's then Cabinet Minister, Shiv Pratap Shukla by a wide margin. Media often quotes that in 2007, Adityanath threatened to field 70 candidates for the State Assembly against the BJP candidates but he reached a compromise in the end. Such pushes and pulls, arguments and counter-arguments; agreements and compromises are a part of any democratically run organization. Calling them strained relationship will be political naivety.

Despite his periodic so-called 'revolts', Yogi Adityanath has a good camaraderie with the RSS and the BJP leaders. BJP stalwarts like L K Advani, RSS chief Mohan Bhagwat and VHP chief Ashok Singhal and many other senior BJP and RSS leaders have often visited Yogi in Gorakhpur.

Subhash Gatade, writing for the People's Democracy, weekly organ of the Communist Party of India (Marxist)[90],

90 The Yogi And The Fanatic. Will Eastern UP Be The Next Gujarat? http://archives.peoplesdemocracy.in/2007/0211/02112007_gatade.htm

states that during 22–24 December 2006, Adityanath organised a three-day *Virat Hindu Mahasammelan* (Grand Hindu Meet) at Gorakhpur at the same time as the BJP National Executive Meet in Lucknow. Gatade tried hard to build a narrative of an obvious conflict between BJP and Yogi. He further adds that despite the 'conflict', several RSS and VHP leaders attended Yogi's *Mahasammelan,* which showed a commitment to pursue the Hindutva goals. What Gatade failed to understand is that many times it could be strategy to test mass acceptance and relevance of certain ideas through strong individual leaders, rather than through the structured party framework.

One more instance often quoted of Yogi's rebellious nature is when Yogi defied the whip culture in the Parliamentary system. In March 2010, Adityanath was one of the several BJP MPs who defied the party whip on the Women's Reservation Bill in the Parliament and said that it was needless. He stated that they were against any reservation and that everybody should come to (the Parliament) on his or her ability. He further added that the BJP leadership had fallen into a trap of the Congress-led government.

When Rajat Sharma of IndiaTV, asked Yogi about his alleged strained relations with BJP in his show 'Aapki Adalat'[91], Yogi said that this question is pointless and claimed that he is completely aligned with the party's philosophy and a five time Member of Parliament on BJP's ticket.

---

91 Yogi Adityanath in Aap Ki Adalat. (2014) https://www.youtube.com/watch?v=WsdqhzaH7qU&t=2390s

Section 3. Yogi Adityanath, as the Mahant of Gorakhdham Mutt

How Ajay Bisht became Yogi Adityanath?

Ajay Bisht, who was studying for a Master's of Science (MSc) in Mathematics in Rishikesh, got distracted from his formal education because of his personal inclination towards the '*Shri Ram Janbhoomi* Movement'. In early 1993, during the peak of the Ram Mandir Movement, he went to Gorakhpur to visit the Gorakhnath Temple and also got the chance to meet Mahant Avaidyanath. Mahant Avaidyanath patiently heard Ajay's story and told him that he was a born *yogi* and was destined to come there one day. This was not Ajay's first interaction with Mahant Avaidyanath. He had briefly met him in 1990, when Mahant was on his India tour for the '*Ram Janmbhoomi*' freedom movement.

In May 1993, Ajay again went to Gorakhpur for a week to meet Mahant Avaidyanath and to express his desire to learn and know more about Yoga. When Ajay was returning, Mahant Avaidyanath asked him to join the Gorakhnath Temple as a full time disciple. Ajay returned with mixed thoughts, but he was immensely influenced by Mahant Avaidyanath[92].

---

92 Rashtra Sant, Mahant Avaidyanath, Publisher: Mahant Avaidyanath Nyas, Gorakhpur

After a couple of months, when Mahant Avaidyanath was admitted in All India Institute of Medical Sciences (AIIMS), New Delhi, for some treatment, Ajay went to see him. At the time, Mahant Avaidyanath earnestly asked Ajay to reconsider his earlier request of joining Gorakhnath Mutt. Mahant Avaidyanath also added that not being in good shape he needed to anoint an able disciple or the *Hindu* community would blame him. So he pressed Ajay further by saying that he saw a natural *yogi* (saint) in him and requested him to join the temple as a disciple. Ajay assured him that by the time Mahant Avaidyanath regained his health and was ready to return to Gorakhpur he would join him there. In November 1993, Ajay left his village, his parents, his friends, and his studies and without disclosing much to anyone in the family, he went to Gorakhpur. On 15 February 1994, on the auspicious occasion of *'basant panchami'*, Ajay was anointed as a *Nath Panth yogi* by his *guru* Mahant Avaidyanath. As destined, Ajay became Yogi Adityanath, Avaidyanath's successor as the Mahant of Gorakhnath Mutt, the oldest Mutt of *Nath Panth*, the tradition, which is said to be originated from Adinath, Lord Shiva.

After the death of Mahant Avaidyanath, on 12 September 2014, Yogi Adityanath became the *Peethadeesh* (head priest) of Gorakhnath temple after a traditional, formal ceremony.

A Day in the Life of Mayant Yogi Adityanath

When I visited Gorakhpur, I noticed that Yogi's twelve-by-twelve room in the Gorakhnath temple just had a bed and a table. As reported by Joydeep Ghosh of Business Standard[93], from personally feeding *gud* (jaggery) to almost 400 cows a day to holding a meeting with locals in the area every morning, Yogi Adityanath, or *baba* as he is popularly called in the area, had given personal attention not only to the

---

93 http://www.business-standard.com/article/opinion/adityanath-as-up-cm-uttam-pradesh-or-yogi-pradesh-117032201500_1.html

Gorakhnath Mutt but to the whole eastern region of Uttar Pradesh.

Yogi Adityanath's aides in the temple told me about his grueling daily schedule that starts at 3am in the morning with his yoga and prayers from 3 to 5 A.M. After a brief *pooja* (prayer) at the temple, he inspects the temple complex for an hour, overseeing all facilities, meeting all staff members and feeding the cows. Then he goes up again to his room at around 6:15 A.M. and reads till around 8:30 A.M. Since he became the *Mahant* (Head Priest) of the temple, his schedule also includes spending an hour signing papers, bills and making other institutional decisions with the senior administrative staff. In between this busy schedule, his barber, Bhagwat Sharma, keeps checking with Yogi Adityanath if he wishes to have a haircut or wants a shave.

Then around 9:30 A.M., he meets people at the Mutt's famous *janta darbar* (people's court), which for decades has been an institution in itself. As further reported by Ghosh, *baba's* followers believe that he can do no wrong and even if he does it then it is considered as done for the larger good. For example, his daily meetings are held without any bias towards the rich or poor, and according to the locals, without any religious bias either. However there is just one condition, which is not to lie to *baba*. The offender is punished by allowing someone else to cultivate his land for months or something even harsher. People waiting to meet *baba* are given *lassi* (butter milk) to keep them nourished.

In these meetings, doles are given out for marriages and for children's education; disputes are resolved and so on. The best part of the *janata darbars* is that they don't end till the last person is heard. A local says that half the disputes get resolved once a party says he or she is going to *baba* for resolution.

By the time I visited the temple for the second time, Yogi Adityanath had become the Chief Minister of Uttar Pradesh, but the *janta darbar* continued at the same pace. Yogi Adityanath's chair was empty, but his close aide from the temple, 65 year-old Dwarka Prasad Tiwari, monitors the complaints of the people and as usual they are followed by a phone call or a letter from the Mutt.

Getting back to *baba's* schedule, it is evident that the entire day's schedule is based on the morning meetings after which *baba* visits the hospital and other parts of the temple complex that need attention. According to the locals, all doctors practicing in the area and other hospitals spend some time every day at the Mutt's hospital and see patients for a nominal fee. Gone are the days when doctors lived under the fear of being kidnapped for ransom – an association with *baba's* temple ensures safety. Similarly, medical shops within the Mutt offer discounts. Some may complain that it is dictatorial, but locals feel that given the high fees of doctors and health care, most people benefit.

Usually after finishing the morning's *janta darbar*, Yogi Adityanath leaves for his constituency, visiting villages, schools, hospitals, institutions, solving issues, disputes, and returns to the temple by 5 or 6 P.M. After coming back he spends time with cows at the *gaushala* (cow' shed) and then goes to his room to freshen up for the evening *pooja* (prayers). After 9 P.M. he meets academicians, principals and other intellectuals up in his room till 10:30 – 11:00 P.M. and only then ends his day.

Pradeep Rao, a close aide of Yogi Adityanath's, while talking about his food habits, told us that Yogi Adityanath rarely gets the time to eat his lunch. Rao added that for them, its like a punishment to accompany him for breakfast or dinner, as his yogic food is too bland for their taste buds. He said that Yogi Adityanath eats fruits, sweet or savory *dalia* (porridge), *chana* (gram) and/or *matha* (butter milk) for his breakfast. For his dinners, or on occasional lunches he eats boiled vegetables with hardly any salt, spices or oil, with some *daal* (lentils), coarse rice and *roti* (Indian bread).

Yogi Adityanath follows, and is making others follow, the same tough schedule even in the Chief Minister's residence and office. The only difference now is that people in his *janta darabar* come from whole of Uttar Pradesh and now he has the state apparatus at his disposal to solve people's issue. Now he also has a whole battery of advisors and bureaucrats to make a statewide systemic policy change for the betterment of the state. However, the fact that a *Nath Panth yogi* (saint) has become the Chief Minister of Uttar Pradesh has still not fully seeped into the political class and bureaucrats in Lucknow.

What is Nath Panth?

To understand Yogi Adityanath, we need to understand *Nath Panth*, its origins, its *gurus* (teachers), its curators, its practices and history.

The Sanskrit word *Nātha* means 'lord' or 'protector'[94]. The related Sanskrit term Adinatha means first or original Lord and is synonymous to Lord Shiva, the founder of the Nāthas. Initiation into the *Nātha sampradaya* includes receiving a name ending in *–Nath*. Like when Mahant Avaidyanath gave *deeksha* (teachings) to 22 year old Ajay in year 1994 and he was named Yogi Aditya-'*Nath*'.

Nath Panth is considered a medieval era movement, which combined ideas from Shaivism, Buddhism and Hatha Yoga traditions of India[95]. Guru Matsyendranātha is considered as the founder of the *Natha Sampradaya*, having received the teachings from Lord Shiva. Guru Matsyendranātha along with his direct disciple Guru Gorakhnath structured and collected all the teachings of *Nath Panth*.

A notable aspect of the Nath tradition practice is its refinements and use of Yoga, particularly Hatha Yoga, to transform one's body into a *Sahaja Siddha* state of awakened self's identity with absolute reality. An accomplished guru, who knows yoga and is a spiritual guide, is considered

94 *Wolf-Dieter Storl (2004). Shiva: The Wild God of Power and Ecstasy. Inner Traditions. p. 258*

95 https://www.britannica.com/topic/Natha

essential, and they have historically been known for their esoteric yogic practices[96].

As per the Mallinson, James' 2011 article on *Nath Sampradaya* states that the *Nāth Sampradāya* today comprises an order of renunciate ascetics and householders, both of which trace their lineages to a group of nine Nāth gurus headed by Ādinātha (First Nāth), who is identified as Lord Shiva. Next, in most lists of nine Nāths, comes Matsyendranātha, followed by Goraksanātha (Gorakhnāth), who is said to have founded the Nāth order of ascetics. The earliest references to the Nāth ascetic order as an organized entity date to the beginning of the 17th century, but its first historical gurus, Matsyendranātha and Goraksanātha, lived much earlier, probably in the 9th and 12th centuries, respectively, and during the intermediate period there are numerous references to both ascetic and householder Nāths in texts, inscriptions, iconography, and historical reports. Guru, Matsyendranātha and Goraksanātha are one of the nine *nathas*, of Shri Nathsampradaya Sidh Parampara, which has 9 *Nathas* and 84 *Sidhas*.

As per the classic book 'Nath Sampradaya' by Hazari Prasad Dwivedi[97], the main sect of Nath Panthi yogis is of Gorakhnathi Yogis. These are also called *'Kanphata'* or *'Darsani' sadhus* (saints). The name *Kanphata* originates from the fact that these yogis pierce their ear and wear a special kind of earring made of mud, ivory or gold. As per Mr Dwivedi, Gorakhnathi *sadhus* are found in various parts of India and are called 'Natha' in Punjab, Bengal, Mumbai and regions of the Himalayas.

The exact number of these sadhus in India over years is quite difficult to find through various census records. George Weston Briggs, in his invaluable book, 'Goraknath and the Kanphata Yogis'[98] attempted to count the number. Briggs

---

96 Mallinson, James (2011) 'NāthSaṃpradāya.' In: Brill Encyclopedia of Hinduism Vol. 3. Brill, pp. 407-428.

97 NathSampradaya' by Hazari Prasad Dwivedi, 1950, Publisher: Hindustan Academy, Uttar Pradesh, Allahabad

98 'Goraknath and the Kanphata Yogis' by George Weston Briggs, 1938, Publisher: Motilal Banarsidass Publishers

said, as per census of 1891, 'Jogis' in India were enumerated at 214,546. The figures from the Provinces of Agra and Oudh for Aughar were 5,319; 28,816 for Gorakhnathi; 78,387 for Jogis, including Gorakhnathi and others. This would indicate that the Gorakhnathi, including Aughars, constituted about 45 percent of Yogis which clearly shows that *Nath Panth* and especially Gorakhnathi Yogis were a sizable portion of India's saint class. The same report for Agra and Oudh, shows that the proportion of male to female Yogis was about 42/35. Some female yogis were widows and some pairs were a family of yogis. Of Yogis reported in Punjab, 38,137 were Muslims. The long history of inclusion of disadvantaged segments of society, like women and Muslim in *Nath Panth,* becomes very important in today's context, when Yogi Adityanath, a *Nath Pantih* yogi has become the Chief Minister of Uttar Pradesh. Even today, many Muslims and women work inside the Gorakhnath Temple and have shops in the temple premise.

Detailing the ear piercing process, among *Kanphate Sadhus,* Briggs wrote that the distinctive marks of the sect of the *Kanphatas* are split-ears and the huge earrings. In the final stage of their ceremony of initiation the central hollows of both ears are split with a two edged knife (or razor) by a specially chosen guru, or teacher. Neem-wood sticks are plugged in and after the wounds have healed, large rings (called mudras) are inserted. These are symbols of the Yogi's faith. Some explain that in splitting the ear a *Nadi* (mystic channel) in the cartilage is cut, thus assisting in acquiring yogic powers. The Yogi wearing the *mudra* (earring) becomes immortal. The rings worn in western India are about 7 inches in circumference and weigh two and a quarter ounces or more. The weight also depends on the substance from which the rings are made of. The rule is that the initiate first wears rings of clay. Some Yogis continue to wear earthen rings, but since these are easily broken they are usually substituted with others made of more durable substance. Rhinoceros horn is a favorite material for earrings. Some important yogis were seen wearing thin gold rings. Other substances used are copper, stag's and antelope's horn, ivory, agate, jade, glass, conch shell and wood. When I was spending time in Gorakhnath temple, while writing this book, I met a Kanphata *sadhu*, who was initiated a couple of days earlier by Yogi Adityanath, head priest of Gorakhnath Mutt. He was wearing big clay mudras (earrings) and his ears were almost dripping with oil, which he told us helps to heal the cut. He told us that a yogi has to follow a tough yogic regime before getting initiated for the ear piercing process. During ear piercing, the yogi is not supposed to shake or cry in pain, failing which he is dropped from the initiation process. Yogi Adityanath is also a *Nath Panthi, Kanpatha sadhu,* who wears a thin gold *mudra* (earring).

There are several temples of the Nath tradition spread across India[99]. Gorakhnath Mutt, named after Guru Gorakhnath is considered one of the most important temples among all the Nath tradition temples across India. To bring all the different sub-sects of Nath tradition together for knowledge sharing and larger camaraderie, one larger forum with the name *Akhil Bhaaratavarsheey Avadhoot Bhesh Baarah Panth Yogee Mahaasabha* is being formed. Yogi Adityanath is the President (*Sabhapati)* of the Mahasabha[100]. The main aim of this organization is to offer assistance to all the Nath yogis and monasteries and to work for the progress of *Nath Sampradaya*. This organization is composed of representatives from the twelve *panths* (branches) of the Nath tradition – Satnathi (Satnath), Ramnathi (Ram ke), Pagal (Pagalpanthi), Pavpanth (Pavak), Dharmnath (Dharmnathi), Mannathi (Manonathi), Kaplani (Kapilpanth), Ganganath (Ganganathi), Nateshvari (Daryanathi), Aaipanth (Aaike), Vairag (Bhartrihari Vairag) and Ravalpanthi.

Guru Gorakhnath

Gorakhpur is the one of the sacred place of worship, meditation and yogic practices of Guru Gorakhnath. He is considered as an avatar of Adinath, Lord Shiva. In Mahakal

99 http://www.gorakhnathmandir.in/mandir-nath-pant-index.html
100 http://yogigorakshnath.org/members-of-sampradaya/

Yogshastra, Lord Shiva Himself said, "I have taken the avatar of Gorakhanath to spread the message of Yog". As per famous author George Weston Briggs[101], Gorakhnath was an influential founder of the *Nath* Hindu monastic movement in India. He is considered one of the two notable disciples of Matsyendranath. His followers are found in India's Himalayan states, the western and central states and the Gangetic plains as well as in Nepal. These followers are called yogis, Gorakhnathi, Darshani or Kanphata.

Gorakhnath is considered a Mahayogi (or great yogi) in the Hindu tradition. He did not emphasize on a specific metaphysical theory or a particular truth, but emphasized that the search for truth and spiritual life is valuable and the normal goal of a man. Gorakhnath championed Yoga, spiritual discipline and an ethical life of self-determination as a means to reach *samadhi* and one's own spiritual truth[102]. His followers are also famous for being a part of the warrior ascetic movement since the 14th-century, to militarily resist persecution against the Islamic and British colonial rule, developing martial arts and targeted response against high officials[103]. Gorakhnath, his ideas and yogis have been highly popular in rural India, with monasteries and temples dedicated to him found in many states of India, particularly in the eponymous city of Gorakhpur. Among urban elites, the movement founded by Gorakhnath has been ridiculed.

Historians vary in their estimate on when Gorakhnath lived. Estimates based on archaeology and text ranges, as Briggs points, from the 11th to 12th century. Baba Farid documents and Jnanesvari manuscripts connects Gorakhnath to the 13th-century. Grierson who relied on the evidence discovered in Gujarat suggests that Gorakhnath lived in

---

101 George Weston Briggs (1938), *Gorakhnath and the Kanphata* Yogis, 6th Edition (2009 Reprint), MotilalBanarsidass. ISBN 978-8120805644

102 AK Banerjea (1983), Philosophy of Gorakhnath with Goraksha-Vacana-Sangraha, ISBN 978-8120805347, page 23-25

103 David Lorenzen (2006), Who Invented Hinduism, Yoda Press, ISBN 978-8190227261, pages 51-63

the 14th century. His influence is found in the numerous references to him in Kabir's poetry and by Guru Nanak in Sikhism, which describe him as a very powerful leader with a large following thereby suggesting he likely lived around the time these spiritual leaders lived in India[104].

Historical texts imply that Gorakhnath was originally a Buddhist in a region influenced by Shaivism, and he converted to Hinduism championing Shiva and Yoga. Gorakhnath led a life as a passionate exponent of ideas of Kumarila and Adi Shankara who championed Yoga and the Advaita Vedanta interpretations of the Upanishads. Gorakhnath considered the controversy between dualism and non-dualism spiritual theories in medieval India useless from practice point of view. He emphasized that the choice is of the yogi, and the spiritual discipline and practice by either leads to "perfectly illumined *samadhi* state of the individual phenomenal consciousness", states Banerjea[105].

Mahant Tradition of Gorakhnath Mutt

Gorakhnath Mutt is the highest center of *Nath Panth*, established with the inspiration of Guru Gorakhnath, disciple of Adinath Lord Shiva. As per the tradition the Mahant of Gorakhnath Mutt is the representative of Guru Gorakhnath. The Mahant tradition of Gorakhnath Mutt is the perfect example of allegiance, integrity and devotion towards the *Guru*. The residence of Mahant of Gorakhdham temple is called 'Shri Gorakshdham Peeth' or 'Mutt'. The Mahant of Gorakhnath Mutt, retains the position of the Mahant for life. All Mahants declare an able disciple as the successor of the Mutt, before their *Samadhi*. And the successor-disciple is anointed as the Mahant of the Gorakhnath Mutt like Mahant Avaidyanath declared his disciple Yogi Adityanath as his successor in 1994. After the *Samadhi* of Mahant Avaidyanath

---

104 George Weston Briggs (1938), *Gorakhnath and the Kanphata* Yogis, 6th Edition (2009 Reprint), MotilalBanarsidass. ISBN 978-8120805644

105 AK Banerjea (1983), Philosophy of Gorakhnath with Goraksha-Vacana-Sangraha, ISBN 978-8120805347, pagea xli, 307-312

in 2014, Yogi Adityanath is anointed as the *Peethadheeshwar* of Gorakhnath Mutt.

Mahant Shri Varadnath is considered the first Mahant of the Gorakhnath Mutt and some famous Mahants after him are – Baba Amritnath, Shri Parmeshwarnath, Shri Budhnath, Shri Ramchandranath, Shri Veernath, Shri Ajabnath, Shri Piyarnath, Shri Baalnath, Shri Maannath, Shri Santoshnath, Shri Meharnath, Shri Gopalnath, Shri Balbhadranath and Shri Dilwarnath. When Shri Dilwarnath was unable to perform his duties Shri Gambhirnath was brought in and along with the Mahant position, was made the guardian of the Gorakhnath temple and Mutt. In 1934 a devoted yogi, and a champion of Hinduism, Mahant Digvijaynath took over as the Mahant of the Mutt, followed by Mahant Avaidyanath.

One of the unique features of the Mahant tradition of Gorakhnath Mutt, is that along with Dharma-Spirituality-Yog, they also value Nationalism. As per the Mutt, Hinduism is Nationalism. Gorakhnath Mutt has unified its yogic traditions and various rituals of Indian tradition. Indian festivals like *Navratra, Vijayadashmi, Shri Ram Abhishek, Holi* etc. have become an integral part of the Mutt's celebrations. Along with Yoga-Spiritualism, people-welfare and service to the people are an important part of the Mutt's activities. Daily *janta darbars* at the Mutt, arrangement of food and butter milk for the destitute, the various education and health related charity institutions run by Gorakhnath Mutt are some of the large scale welfare initiatives undertaken by the Mutt.

Welfare Activities of Gorakhnath Mutt

Gorakhnath Mutt has always given importance to social welfare along with religion and spirituality. The Mutt expanded its social welfare activities[106] exponentially under the leadership of Mahant Digvijaynath[107].

---

106 *Shri Gorakhnath MandirEvam Gorakhpur kaItihas, Published by: Shri Gorakhnath Mandir*

107 http://164.100.47.194/Loksabha/Members/MemberBioprofile.aspx?mpsno=7

Welfare activities in the Education field

In 1932, Mahant Digvijaynath established Maharana Pratap Education Council in Gorakhpur. Mahant Digvijaynath comes from Rajasthan and was influenced by the valor of the brave Maharana Pratap. In 1946 Mahant Digvijaynath established the Maharana Pratap College and the Maharana Pratap Women's College. In 1958, the Mutt merged both these institutions to pave way for the formation of Gorakhpur University. Maharana Pratap Education Council runs more than 44 education institutions today in the field of primary, secondary and higher education. More than 50,000 girls and boys study technology courses, Sanskrit, graduation courses, polytechnic and nursing courses in these Mutt's institutions. Along with the regular course content, these students are also taught Indian culture, tradition and nationalism.

Conservation of Sanskrit Language and Indian Culture

The Mutt has done phenomenal work in the field of conservation of Sanskrit language and the Indian culture. Within the premises of the Gorakhnath Mutt, there is a Sanskrit Language College, affiliated to Sampoornanand Sanskrit University and almost 300 students study there. There is also a hostel within the temple premise and all the expenses of these students are borne by the Gorakhnath Temple administration.

Medical Education and Hospital

The Mutt played a crucial role in establishing the medical facilities in the region. In 1972, the Mutt established the Gorakshnath Ayurvedic College and the Digvijaynath Ayurvedic Hospital. Though the Ayurvedic College had to be closed in 1984, Digvijaynath Ayurvedic Hospital is functioning. Over years this Ayurvedic hospital was further modernized. In 2003, a modern Gorakshnath Hospital was established, equipped with advance medical devices and has become a boon for the poor people of Bihar, Eastern Uttar Pradesh and lowland areas of Nepal. This became a good alternative for the people of the region, to the dying government medical infrastructure and costly private hospitals. The Mutt also organizes regular medical camps in villages and helps bring medical assistance to the doorstep of the poor, who are unable to come to the hospital.

The Guru Gorakhnath School of Nursing is engaged in training para-medical staff, crucial for medical establishments. The Mutt is also planning to start a medical college named Guru Gorakhnath Institute of Medical Sciences.

Food for the Poor

Twice a day, the Mutt organizes a large *Bhandara* (Serving free food for masses) for thousands of saints, poor and homeless people. This is the philosophy of *Nath* tradition- no one should go hungry from the Mutt. There are no questions asked to receive food at the Mutt. People from any caste and religion can just join the *bhandara* with reverence and they will be fed.

Raring of Cows

There is a well-organized *Gaushala* (Cow Shed) within the premises of the Gorakhnath Mutt, where hundreds of cows, calves and bulls are raised. The Mutt propagates the message of their love for cows and their love of animals through their actions. Spending time with cows is an essential part of Yogi Adityanath's routine, during his stay in Gorakhpur. Buttermilk made from the milk from these cows is served as a *prasad* (God's sacred offering) in the Mutt to the disciples and visitors.

Yoga Center

Gorakhnath Mutt gives great important to Yoga. In India, Maharishi Patanjali and Shri Gorakshnathji, are the pioneers of two parallel streams of Yoga. Gorakhnath Mutt is actively involved in the philosophy and practical aspects of Yoga. Every year the Mutt organizes a Seven Day National Yoga Camp. The Mutt also conducts daily yoga classes, free of cost for the people of the area.

Library

Gorakhnath Temple has an incredible library with a wide range of collections of books on Philosophy of Yoga, Nath tradition and Indian tradition. The library also has many old manuscripts related to Nath tradition. The library also maintains all the editions of the 'Yogvani' magazine published by the Mutt. The library stocks all the books published by the Mutt over years. Gorakhnath Temple also has its own publication division, which has already published more than three dozen important books.

Communal and social harmony drives

The Gorakhnath temple respects the diversity within the Hindu religion. In the temple, along with the statues of Gurus of Nath tradition, they have statues of all the important Gods and Goddesses of Hinduism. The temple is determined to work towards social harmony in the society and against caste and class based differences and untouchability. Mahant Avaidyanath played a crucial role towards this drive. He frequently visited villages and ate with people from different castes. He ate with the Dom King of Kashi, along with the other saints, and facilitated the anointment of many *dalits* as the priests and Mahants of different temples.

Camps, Seminars and Conventions

The Gorakhnath temple organizes regular camps, seminars and conventions on religion, philosophy, spirituality, yoga, culture and other similar themes. Since 1970, Mutt organizes a special seven-day event, which combines a *dharma sansad* (Religion Parliament) and *jan sansad* (People's Parliament), that covers topics related to religion and people.

Janta Darabars

Janta darbars organized by Gorakhnath Mutt are very popular among the people in whole of eastern Uttar Pradesh. People take their problems to the Mutt and get them sorted out. After taking over as the Chief Minister of Uttar Pradesh, Yogi Adityanath has started the *janta darbars* in Lucknow also, while the *janata darbars* in the Mutt are still continued by Mutt's senior staff.

History of Gorakhpur and Mutt's role in its Development

Gorakhpur has had the good fortune of being the sacred land, once occupied by Guru Gorakhnath for his meditation and prayers. Guru Gorakhnath must have selected this place, near river Rapti (erstwhile name Iravati), as it was, isolated, uninhabited jungle suitable for peaceful yogic meditation and there are a few references of inhabitation in Gorakhpur. As per a known reference, the King of Stati from Rudrapur (in the Deoria district), Vishram Singh was childless. He adopted the prince of Unval (in Gorakhpur district), Mangal Singh. Mangal Singh established a small town, south of the place of worship of Guru Gorakhnath, called Gorakhpur.

Before being named Gorakhpur, this region was part of an ancient Indian civilization and was witness to the development of dharma, culture, development of new administrative systems and political journey of the region. This region has had the honor to be the part of Ikshvaku dynasty of Ayodhya and witnessed the rule of Lord Rama. This place has hosted Mahabali Bheem, who came to invite Guru Gorakhnath for the Rajasuya *yajna* (sacrifice) performed by King Yudhisthira. In fact the current Gorakhnath Temple premise, has a giant lying statue of Mahabali Bheem, depicting the incident. This place has witnessed the rise and fall of Shavites of Kapilavastu, during the times of Lord Budha. This region was part of the great kingdom of Chandragupta II Vikramaditya and King Harsh.

Gorakhpur came under attack during the Mughal rule. During Aurangzeb's rule, Prince Muazam came to hunt in this region and setup a Mughal base there. He changed the name to Muazamabad. Later the region came under British rule, but owning to longstanding local history of being the sacred land of Guru Gorakhnath, the original name Gorakhpur prevailed over years. In his interviews Yogi Adityanath often states that over the years many original names of various places were changed by Muslim invaders. Yogi is infamous for changing these names back to their original names. When Yogi became an MP, there used to be a market called Mia Bazar that he christened to its original name, Maya Bazar. Similarly Urdu Bazar was renamed back to Hindi Bazar and Ali Nagar again became Arya Nagar.

In 1869, Gorakhpur became a grade three Municipal area. In 1885, Gorakhpur was connected by a railway line. In 1891, the place became the headquarters of a commissionary. After independence, in 1948 Gorakhpur became a grade two Municipal area. In 1923, the famous Geeta Press was established in Gorakhpur and because of Geeta Press, Gorakhpur got the reputation of a place that works for publication and spread of Hinduism, culture and tradition. By 1956, with the population of 1,50,000, Gorakhpur became a grade one Municipal area. In their drive to setup an alternative system of education Rashtriya Swamsevak Sangh (RSS), established the first Saraswati Shishu Mandir in Gorakhpur in 1952. The first private polytechnic of the country was established by the Maharana Pratap Education Council in 1956 and in 1962 Mandan Mohan Malviya College of Engineering was established. In 1963, a big fertilizer factory was established. In 1968 Baba Raghav Das Medical College was established in Gorakhpur and in year 1973 Digvijaynath Ayurvedic Medical College was established within the premise of Gorakhnath Mutt. In 1974 Akashvani Radio services were started in Gorakhpur. In 1977 Gorakhpur Development Authority was established, due to which Gorakhpur's urban development accelerated. In 1982 Gorakhpur became a full-fledged Municipality and in 1994 it was declared a Municipal Corporation. Recently due to efforts of Yogi Adityanath, the fertilizer plant that has remained closed since 1990 restarted and Gorakhpur is all set to get an AIIMS. The Mutt's role was integral in the spiritual, social and administrative development of Gorakhpur. Gorakhpur was urbanizing, but the tenants of *Nath Path*, like waking up early, practicing yoga, daily prayers and living with mutual cooperation became part of Gorakhpur's culture.

Mutt's role in Ram Mandir Andolan

Ram Janmbhoomi Andolan brought unity of various castes and sub-sects of Hinduism. All Hindus came together for a larger cause of national cultural pride. *Ram Janmbhoomi Andolan* helped the Bhartiya Janta Party immensely to uncover the blatant Muslim appeasement done by Congress and other regional parties at the cost of the Hindu majority. It also led to consolidation of votes for Bhartiya Janta Party, starting from early 1990s. Mahants of the Gorakhnath Mutt played a very crucial role in leading *Ram Janmbhoomi Andolan* from the front.

Gorakhnath Temple produced high quality literature on the historical facts related to *Ram Janmbhoomi*[108]. As per the Mutt's literature, King Kush made a grand temple in Ayodhya, the birthplace of his father Lord Rama. Later king Vikaramaditya of Gupta Empire renovated it further. In the following years, various Muslim invaders tried sabotaging it with Salar Masood, brother-in-law of Mahmood Ghaznavi, making two unsuccessful attempts. Muhammad Ghori led the most brutal attacks on the Ram Temple structure, but it remained intact. Mughal invader Babar ordered his deputy Meer Baqi to break the ancient temple structure and build a mosque over it. Meer Baqi used the might of Mughal forces and broke the temple structure and built a Mosque. Since then various attempts were being made to free up *Ram Janmbhoomi* from this disputed structure built by Babar.

In 1949, Mahant Digvijaynath took cognizance of the Ram Temple issue in its entirety and joined Akhil Bharatiya Ramayana Mahasabha. Akhil Bharatiya Ramayana Mahasabha organized a nine-day long recitation of the *Ramcharitmanas* in front of the disputed structure built by the Muslim invaders, which ended with placement statues of Lord Rama and Goddess Sita inside the disputed structure. Mahant Digvijaynath worked closely with Swami Karpatriji,

---

108 Rashtra Sant Mahant Avaidyanath, Published by Mahant Avaidyanath Trust

founder of Akhil Bhartiya Dharma Sangh, to build the initial momentum around *Ram Janmbhoomi.*

A couple of decades later, on 21 July, 1984, the *Shri Ram Janmbhoomi Yagna Samiti* was formed in a meeting of all saints of India in Valmiki Bhavan in Ayodhya for reinvigorating the *Ram Janmbhoomi Andolan* movement. Mahant Avaidyanath was unanimously appointed as the President of the *Samiti*. He remained the President of the *Samiti* all his life.

In a second Dharma-Sansad (Religion Parliament) organized on 1 November, 1985, an ultimatum was given to the government, to open the locks of *Shri Ram Janmbhoomi* by 8 March, 1986, or face a movement by lakhs of saints and their disciples. Mahant Avaidyanath was appointed as the coordinator for this all India movement. With the combined efforts of Mahant Avaidyanath, Vishwa Hindu Parishad (VHP) and a young lawyer from Faizabad, this movement was able to secure a court order to open the doors of *Shri Ram Janmbhoomi* on 1 February, 1986. The movement was able to put enough pressure on Rajiv Gandhi, the then Prime Minister of India, to co-opt him in the decision.

In the third Dharma-Sansad in Prayag (Allahabad), on 9 November, 1989 under the leadership of Mahant Avaidyanath, it was decided to collect a worshiped brick and one rupee twenty-five paisa from each Hindu across lakhs of villages of India for *Shri Ram Janmbhoomi* movement. On 1 February 1989, during the *Kumbh Mela* in Prayag, the speech of famous Devraha Baba, further enthused the Hindus. Devraha Baba emphasized again that *Shri Ram Janmbhoomi* belongs to Hindus and the Ram Temple must be built there.

On 22 September, 1989, a Mega Hindu Convention was organized, under the leadership of Mahant Avaidyanath at the Boat Club in New Delhi. The following resolutions were passed in the Convention – *Shri Ram Janmbhoomi* always belonged to Hindus and will remain so forever; for the construction of a grand temple at *Shri Ram Janmbhoomi*, the foundation stone will be laid on 9 November, 1989;

Shri Ram Janmbhoomi will be an electoral issue in the upcoming elections and those against it will be voted out of power.

The then Home Minister of India, Buta Singh and the then Chief Minister of Uttar Pradesh Narayan Dutt Tiwari tried hard to convince Mahant Avaidyanath to delay the foundation stone laying ceremony, but Mahant Avaidyanath was determined. On 9 November, 1989 the foundation stone laying ceremony started with full Vedic rituals and on 10 November, 1989, Shri Kamleshwar Prasad, a Schedule Caste, laid the foundation stone. On this grand occasion Mahant Avaidyanath said, this was not just the foundation stone laying of Shri Ram Temple, but is the foundation stone laying of the path to a Hindu nation, the foundation stone laying of the unity of the Hindu society and of social harmony in Hindu society.

After the foundation stone laying ceremony, the *Shri Ram Janmbhoomi* movement had reached a different height. The then Prime Minister Vishwanath Pratap Singh met Mahant Avaidyanath and assured him of some concrete action in next four months. This proved to be just a time buying tactic by the Prime Minister. Prime Minister Vishwanath Pratap Singh attempted to break the momentum of the *Shri Ram Janmbhoomi* movement, by bringing in Mandal Commission, to create a divide within the Hindu society. Mulayam Singh Yadav, the then Chief Minister of Uttar Pradesh, started naming *Shri Ram Janmbhoomi* movement as a communal movement and started harassing saints and volunteers of the Rashtriya Swamsevak Sangh (RSS) throughout the state.

Shri Ram Janmbhoomi movement committee had declared 30 October, 1990 as the date for mega gathering of *Kar Sevaks* (volunteers for religious missions) in Ayodhya. The Mulayam government claimed to make full proof arrangement to stop anyone from entering Ayodhya. On 26 October, Mahant Avaidyanath was arrested on his way from Delhi to Ayodhya, but despite all the arrangements by the state government, lakhs of *Kar Sevaks* entered Ayodhya on 30 October. Irritated by their failure, Mulayam government ordered indiscriminate firing on the *Kar Sevaks,* which lead to the death of many *Kar Sevaks*. For the next whole year countrywide demonstrations happened against the firing on *Kar Sevaks* by the Mulayam government. Next year, on 30 October, 1991, Shaurya Divas (Valor Day) was organized at Ayodhya. On this occasion Mahant Avaidyanath said, the construction of a grand temple at the *Shri Ram Janmbhoomi* would happen by virtue of the valor of Hindus and not by anyone's mercy.

On 23 July, 1992 a delegation met Prime Minister PV Narsimha Rao, under the leadership of Mahant Avaidyanath. This was Mahant's third meeting with the Prime Minister PV Narsimha Rao on the topic of *Shri Ram Janmbhoomi.* Mahant Avaidyanath agreed to Prime Minister's request of suspending the work for three months to arrive at an agreeable solution. Three months passed, but nothing happened.

On 30 October, 1992, the fifth Dharma-Sansad was organized. The Dharma-Sansad decided 6 December, 1992, as the date to start the work of temple construction (*Kar Seva)* at the site of *Shri Ram Janmbhoomi*. Following the grand appeal of saints of India, on 6 December, 1992, lakhs of *Kar Sevaks* gathered again in Ayodhya. In the presence of Mahant Avaidyanath, renowned saints of different Hindu organizations and important leaders of Bhartiya Janta Party, the disputed structure was demolished to debris within no time. Though, many political events unfolded following the demolition of the disputed structure at Ayodhya, Mahant Avaidyanath was contented that the birthplace of Lord Rama was freed from the offensive structure, built after demolishing the Rama Temple.

Mahant Avaidyanath continued the movement in different capacities for the next two decades, till he died in 2014. Yogi Adityanath joined him in 1994 and raised the issue of *Ram Janmbhoomi* multiple times in the Parliament. With Bhartiya Janta Party government at both center and Uttar Pradesh, now there is big hope for a grand temple of Lord Rama in Ayodhya.

What Changed at *Ram Janmbhoomi* after Yogi became CM

Atul Chandra, wrote a detailed account in Swarajya[109], with the title – "*This Is What Has Changed At Ram Janmabhoomi Since Adityanath Took Over As UP Chief Minister*". As per Atul, Union Government has already allocated Rs 154 crore for the construction of a Ramayan museum. After taking charge, Yogi government cleared 20 acres of land required for the Museum. The state government also upgraded the Ayodhya civic body to the level of a municipal corporation. Orders have also been issued for the revival of Ramleela in Ayodhya.

A day after the CBI court charged senior BJP leaders L K Advani, M M Joshi and others in May, Yogi Adityanath became the first Uttar Pradesh Chief Minister in 15 years to pray at the makeshift Ram temple. Although, he did not talk about the temple during his visit, he announced Rs 350 crore for sprucing up the pilgrim city while assuring its residents of "uninterrupted Ramleela", reported Atul.

As per Atul Chandra of Swarajya, these developments must be viewed along with the arrival of stones for the proposed temple. On 21 June 2017, two trucks carrying huge stones reached Ayodhya for use in the proposed Ram temple. A little over a fortnight later, on 5 July morning, three more truckloads of stones reached Ayodhya, while six more were on their way. According to Sharad Sharma, the VHP spokesperson, there were 110,000 cubic feet of stones cut and carved for use in the proposed temple. Work at the "karyashala" (workshop) in Ayodhya has continued uninterrupted over the years, Sharma said. Although the present quantity "is sufficient to build the ground floor", another 70,000 cubic feet were required for the construction

109 https://swarajyamag.com/politics/this-is-what-has-changed-at-ram-janmabhoomi-since-yogi-took-over

of the first floor, he added. In 2015, the Samajwadi Party government had stopped the transportation of stones to Ayodhya inviting condemnation from the Vishwa Hindu Parishad (VHP).

Section 4.
Yogi Adityanath, as Ajay Bisht of Uttarakhand

The phenomenon called Yogi Adityanath did not happen in a day. The persona of today's Yogi Adityanath has shown impressions of it from his early upbringing. There is very little that is known of Yogi Adityanath's pre-Gorakhpur days – his upbringing, his schooling, his college days, about his family and friends. Collecting these missing pieces of the puzzle for my readers, took me to the hills of Uttarakhand.

Ajay's birth in *Devbhoomi*, Uttarakhand

Yogi Adityanath was born as Ajay Mohan Singh Bisht on 5 June 1972 in a village called Masalgaon in Uttarkhashi district of Uttar Pradesh (now in Uttarakhand), while his father was posted there. He was the fifth born in the family, among four brothers and three sisters. His father, Anand Singh Bisht, was a forest ranger and his mother Savitri Devi, was a homemaker. It's interesting to note that in his electoral forms Yogi Adityanath fills Mahant Avaidyanath's name under the father's name, as after *Sanyas,* the Guru is considered the father.

During my discussion with Ajay Bisht's biological father, Shri Anand Singh Bisht, he told me that he worked tirelessly and with honesty in the Forest Department for 38 years. In his service that panned for four decades, he worked in the

Mussoorie division, Tons division, Uttarkhashi division, Tihri division and retired from Pauri division in 1991. He said that he was not one of those officers who accumulated a lot of money through corruption and built houses, during different postings, because of which his children are righteous and honest. He further added that his family lived in Pauri Garhwal for the larger part of his career, while he was posted to different places. In fact most of Ajay's upbringing happened in their native village, Panchur, in Pauri Garhwal. Panchur is a small village with around 15-20 households and is part of Thangar Gram Panchayat of Yamkeshwar block in Uttarakhand.

Ajay's mother Savitri Devi ji told me that Ajay was quite fond of his three older sisters. In a recent interview on India TV, Yogi Adityanath mentioned that he has learnt a lot from his sisters. Yogi said that his sisters were the ones who introduced him to his first *Akshar Gyan* (alphabet knowledge), and language. While talking about Ajay, Savitri Devi ji also gave details of her other children as well. She had three girls -Pushpa Bisht, Kaushalya Bisht and Sashi Bisht, followed by four boys Manendra Singh Bisht, Ajay Singh Bisht, Shailendra Singh Bisht and Mahendra Singh Bisht. She further said that, Pushpa, who was married in a nearby village, Badoli in Yamkeshwar, lives in the National Capital Region, Kaushalya lives in Kotdwar in Uttarakhand and Sashi lives in Neelkhant in Uttarakhand. Out of her sons, Manendra works as a computer operator cum teacher in Guru Gorakhnath College near the Panchur village set up under Yogi Adityanath's guidance and run directly by the Gorakhnath Mutt. Shailendra works as *Subedar* in Garhwal Rifles in Indian Army serving the country. Mahendra, her youngest son is a journalist with Amar Ujala newspaper and also teaches in a school. And, "Ajay, you all know", she proudly concluded the list.

Savitri Devi ji also told me that Ajay was good student and never kept bad company. She said that he was a simple boy and they never realized that he would grow to this stature. She fondly remembered how close he was to her as his father was usually posted at different locations and he was also strict, so all the children were a little scared of him. Regarding their personal habits, Savitri Devi ji said that everyone in their house always woke up early. Even at the age of around 80, she still wakes up at 4 A.M. to finish her chores and then goes to the fields to oversee the small agriculture farms that they have. At 85, Ajay's father also gets up at 4 A.M. everyday and cleans the whole house and the surrounding compound. Savitri Devi ji said that right from his childhood, Ajay was fond of cows. The Bisht family had cows at home and taking them out to graze was part of Ajay's routine after school. Pointing to the trees around their house in Panchur, Savitri Devi ji told me that Ajay had planted many of these, when he was a boy. Today, Yogi Adityanath lives a yogic life, but his *sanskaras* of waking up before sunrise, his love for cows, his respect for nature and the environment, his complete alignment with PM Narendra Modi's *Swachh Bharat Abhiyan*, his strong stand against corruption and his utmost respect for women, seems to have developed and was nurtured in his formative years by his parents.

Shri Anand Singh Bisht said that Ajay was always polite and courteous and was an avid newspaper reader right from a very young age. Shri Bisht said that although he was constantly on tours and often away from home, he made it a point to check on his children and gave surprise visits to ensure their diligence and attention to studies. He said that maybe owing to all this today, the Ajay of Panchur has become Yogi Adityanath, 21st Chief Minister of Uttar Pradesh. It's interesting to note that, after becoming the Chief Minister of Uttar Pradesh, Yogi and his Ministers have conducted a series of 'surprise checks' of delivery of different government services. Shri Bisht is a proud father who feels that managing a state like UP, is not everybody's cup of tea and only Yogi can control it because since his childhood he has developed a good ability to make decisions. Shri Bisht also told me that Yogi's work as a Member of Parliament was always for the people and free from any type of corruption and that's why people love him. He further added that his life has changed a little bit after his son has become the Chief Minister of UP. People have started flocking for his *sifarish (recommendations)* to his son. He keeps such people at bay by graciously accepting their congratulations and asking them to join him for tea while politely telling them that no recommendations will be entertained. Shri Bisht said that as a forest ranger, he has worn a Khakhi dress all his life. His uniform had three stars on the shoulders, which looked like a police uniform, and moreover, his uniform also had a UPF (Uttar Pradesh Forest) badge, which was quite similar to UPP (Uttar Pradesh Police) badge and this sometimes scared Ajay's friends as they mistook him for a policeman. He laughed and added that now after Ajay has become CM, he has, with him, a full time Khakhi dressed gunman, a real policeman, as part of the security protocol.

Ajay's initial schooling at Thangar, Chamakhot and Gaja

During my visit to Panchur village, I met Deepak Chandra of the same village, who was two years junior to Ajay Bisht in school. While talking with Deepak I discovered that Ajay Bisht went to the Government Primary School in Thangar for his primary schooling. Panchur village is part of Thangar Gram Panchayat of the Yamkeshwar Block. Deepak said that Ajay was a silent boy, but was always eager to help the people around him. As the government school in Thangar was only till grade 8, Ajay had to move to another government school at Chamakhot for his 9th grade and to Gaja, in Tihri, for his 10th grade[110] education.

The Professor of History, at the Mahayogi Guru Gorkhnath College, in Yamkeshwar, Dr. Umesh Tyagi, said that the Yamkeshwar area has a history of producing, spiritual and nationalist marvels. As per Bhishma Kukreti, the local folk story[111] behind Yamkeshwar Temple is amazing and today

110 https://www.youtube.com/watch?v=_xfvd0R9ZMI

111 Bhishma Kukreti, 1984, Garhwal Ki Lok Kathayen, Binsar Prakashan

Yamkeshwar is a renowned Shiva Temple in Uttarakhand. Yamkeshwar is situated on the banks of *Sated* or *Satedi* River (Satyabhama or Satyarudra River) and is surrounded by a *Shamsan* (cremation field) on the remaining three corners. The story, behind Yamkeshwar Mahadev Temple, goes that a great sage Maharishi Mrikand who lived in the area with his wife Marudmati worshipped Shiva and sought from him the boon of begetting a son. As a result, he was given the choice of either a gifted son, but with a short life on earth or a child of low intelligence, but with a long life. Mrikandu *rishi* chose the former, and was blessed with Markandeya, an exemplary son, destined to die at an early age. Lord Narad, by the study of astrology, predicted that Markandeya would die by his eleventh year, which naturally made Mrikand sad. Markandeya asked for remedies to get a longer life and on Sage Mrikand's suggestion Markandeya went to Manikut hill plateau and started *Tap* (prayer) of Maha Mrityunjaya Jap on the banks of Shatrudra River. Markandeya molded an idol of Shiva in sand and started his *Jap* (prayer) under a Peepal tree. On the set day of death for Markandeya, Yamraj (the death God) reached to take his life. But Markandeya requested Yamraj to wait as his *Jap* of Maha Mrityunjaya (a religious ritual for winning over death) was still incomplete. However, Yamraj threw his *Kalpash* (death weapon) on Markandeya. But Markandeya held the sand idol of Lord Shiva in his hands that was struck by the weapon and from the broken idol Maha Mrityunjaya Rudra emerged. Watching Lord Shiva appear, Yamraj ran towards Jamradi village (today's Yamkeshwar). Yamraj started doing *Jap* for lord Shiva (of Shiva's Maha Mrityunjaya Rudra form) at Jamradi. Lord Shiva told Yamraj that wherever there is a Maha MrityunJaya Jap (ritual), Yamraj should not enter there. Lord Shiva also told Yamraj that where he (Yamraj) was performing *Jap*, there was a self-born *ling* and Lord Shiva suggested to Yamraj to perform *Jap* or prayer of that self-born Ling. Lord Shiva proclaimed that the self-born *ling* would be famous by name of Yama. Lord Shiva said that whoever performs the prayer of Yama Shiv Ling would be blessed with a long life. Yamraj performed

Jap of lord Shiva or *Ishwar* for a year there and thus, the place came to be called Yamkeshwar. The nearby villages of Thangar, Panchur, Kandi, Damrana, Bithyani have a deep religious and spiritual influence of Yamkeshwar. Ajay Bisht, who was brought up in Panchur village had these powerful and spiritual folklores as a part of his life.

Yamkeshwar has also had importance in the *Shilpkar* Liberation Movement in Garhwal in 1931, where a conference was held by *Shilpkars* to eradicate untouchability from the society. A nearby village, named Kandi, located near Panchur, has historically been politically very active and has been called the political capital of the region. During India's freedom movement, when Govind Ballabh Pant called upon the youth of the nation to work at the grassroots level in their respective hometowns, BHU student Jagmohan Singh Negi, left BHU to join the freedom movement, in his village in Uttarakhand. In Damrana, Kranti Chandra Uniyal, a Bachelor of Ayurveda, Medical and Surgery (BAMS) from Rishikul Medical College, Rishikesh, left his important degree and profession mid-way to devote his life to India's freedom movement. There are almost 26 recorded freedom fighters from this area, who have contributed immensely to India's freedom movement. This area was declared as *baaghi* (a place of rebels) by the British rulers. It's not a surprise that we see the same rebel nature in Yogi Adityanath as well. Kandi is also the birthplace of Mahant Avaidyanath, who left his house at a very early age and became a *Nath Panthi* saint. Years later, Mahant Avaidyanath found Ajay and in him found a true successor for the Gorakhnath Mutt. Ajay was brought up in the resonance of these spiritual and nationalist personalities and we see the same set of qualities in him today.

Ajay's schooling in Rishikesh

For his 11th and 12th grades Ajay moved to Rishikesh, a town in Uttarakhand where he enrolled in Shri Bharat Mandir Inter College and opted to study the PCM (Combination of

Physics, Chemistry and Mathematics) along with English and Hindi. In Rishikesh, Ajay lived with his elder brother Manendra, who at the time was completing his graduation from a college there.

When I visited the school, Ajay's former Hindi teacher, Shri Bansi Dhar Pokhriyal, Physical Training teacher, Shri DPS Rawat, and Mathematics teacher, Shri Devendra Kumar Varshney, proudly showed me the classrooms where Ajay used to sit. While discussing Yogi Adityanath's oratory skills, Shri Pokhriyal told me that Ajay was a very good orator even in school. The School used to organize *Vad-Vivad Manch* (Debating Platform) every week where Ajay regularly participated.

Shri Varshney said that Ajay was a curious child and asked many questions. Mr Varshney was also the Chief Proctor of the school and maintaining discipline in the school was one of his responsibilities. He remembered Ajay often reporting to him, on students who engaged in bad habits like smoking.

"We both had exactly the same name and that used to create confusion for the teachers", said a classmate at Bharat Mandir Inter College who shares the same name – Ajay Bisht. Ajay's namesake, who now works closely with Member of Parliament, Ramesh Pokhriyal 'Nishank', told me that during the 2014 parliamentarian oath taking ceremony, he was accompanying Nishank ji. He spotted Yogi Adityanath and introduced him as his former classmate. He said Yogi recognized him immediately and gave him a big hug.

Shri Pokhriyal mentioned that it's not a mere coincidence that this school is also being run under the Mahant tradition. Mahants of Bharat Mandir Trust run this school and some other institutions around Rishikesh, for the welfare of the local people. Bharat Mandir is linked to Shri Bharat, brother of Lord Rama. Shri Pokhriyal referenced that in Ramayana, after killing Ravana, Lord Rama and his brother were considered sinners, as Ravana was a Vedic Brahmin. To get rid of that sin, all the brothers came to Rishikesh. Ram Ji did a *pooja* (prayer) in a place called Devprayag. Now Devprayag has a Raghunath Temple in the name of Lord Rama. Laxmanji suffered from leprosy as a result of the curse of killing so many people in the war. Laxmanji did *pooja* (prayer) near River Ganga and took a bath everyday in a hot water source in Ganga that got him rid of leprosy. That place is now famous as 'Laxman Jhula'. Shatrughan ji has a temple near 'Muni Ki Reti' in Rishikesh, as he prayed there. Bharat ji had the least sin among all the brothers so he did a *pooja* (prayer) of Lord Vishnu in Rishikesh. Vishnu ji gave him a boon, that wherever he prayed would be named after him. There is a grand Bharat Temple at the place and is the sole temple in his name in the whole country. Vishnu Ji is also worshipped as Rishikesh Narayan and so this place is called Rishikesh after him.

Over years Bharat Mandir Trust has been very active in social welfare activities. In 1920,the trust established Shri Bharat Sanskrit Vidyalaya. Coincidently, Yogi Adityanath's guru, Mahant Avaidyanath ji was also educated in Sanskrit Education from the same school. In 1942, Mahant Parshuram of Bharat Mandir Trust established the Bharat Mandir Inter College, for students from 6th to grade 12th, where Ajay did his intermediate studies. Even today this is one of the biggest schools in the area. Around 2002, Bharat Mandir Trust started a CBSE School at the Bharat Mandir Temple compound. Bharat Mandir Trust also established the Jyoti Special School for specially abled children. In 1972, Lalit Mohan Sharma of Bharat Mandir Trust donated a large piece of land to the state government to start a Degree College. Over the years the government developed it as Pandit Lalit Mohan Sharma Government PG College. Incidentally, after his graduation from Kotdwar, Ajay enrolled for his Master of Science studies in Mathematics from Pandit Lalit Mohan Sharma Government PG College, Rishikesh. However he did not complete his Masters as it was during this time that he moved to the Gorakhnath Mutt to live the life of a *Nath Panthi Sanyasi*. It is noteworthy that today Gorakhnath Mutt runs more than 44 different educational institutions under the leadership of Mahant Yogi Adityanath in the eastern Uttar Pradesh for the welfare of the people. Shri Pokhriyal also told me that in the hills of Uttarakhand, the *Nath* tradition and stories of *Kanphate Sadhus* is part of folklore. Srinagar, Garhwal has a grand temple of *Nath* tradition. Even Rishikesh, and Haridwar has temples of *Nath* tradition.

Ajay's college days in Kotdwar

In 1989, Ajay joined PG Government College in Kotdwar, to pursue his graduation. He opted for the PCM group again as he had graduated his intermediate in the same subjects. In Kotdwar, I heard some interesting anecdotes about Ajay's formative years, which gives us an insight into Ajay's thinking process and personality.

Anil Bhist, classmate of Ajay told us that, Raj Bhushan Singh Rawat, Anil Bisht, Sandeep Bisht, Anoop Kandari, Harshpal Rana, Arvind Bansal, Neeraj Agarwal and three girls named Babita Rana, Saraswati Rawat and Aarti Dhondhiyal were a part of the group that Ajay used to hangout with in the college. Raj Bhushan Singh Rawat still works very closely with Yogi Adityanath and has also moved to Lucknow, after Yogi became Chief Minister. Raj Bhushan Singh Rawat, also known as Raja Babu, also organizes regular college reunions and is the contact point for the all the classmates to reach out to their former classmate, Chief Minister Yogi Adityanath.

Neeraj Aagarwal, one of Ajay classmates, who now runs a jewellery shop in Kotdwar, told me that the whole group including Ajay, used to run 3 kms everyday in the morning from Jhanda Chauk in Kotdwar to Sidhbali Hanuman Temple. Then the group used to play Badminton and Ajay would practice yoga and regularly followed his exercise routine. The whole group often used to plan picnics in nearby places like, Kala Garh, Tadkeshwar and Mussoorie. Kotdwar was a big city and Ajay was fully independent. Though Ajay was simple and reserved, he also tried to catch up with the trends of the city. In some of the college pictures, Ajay was seen sporting goggles and bandanas.

While talking about Ajay, another classmate Babita Rana told us that Ajay was quite reserved by nature, but always eager to help his classmates. Babita narrated that in their first year in college, one of their classmates, Saraswati Rawat, stood for the position of Joint Secretary in the college student elections and their group, including Ajay, went to an area called Duggada for her election canvassing. By the time they had finished their campaign it was almost 6 P.M. and none of the buses stopped for them as college students were notorious for taking the bus without paying for the ticket. Unfortunately bus was the only mode of transportation to get back to Kotdwar city and it was getting dark. As there were no mobile phones in those days there was no way for the students to inform their concerned families at home. Babita got too worried thinking that her parent's would be upset and may not allow her to enter the house. Babita was almost in tears and noticed that all of a sudden, Ajay stood in front of the next bus forcing it to stop. The bus stopped, just inches away from Ajay. Everyone was concerned for Ajay's safety, but he did not pay heed to the conductor's resistance and first asked all girls to quickly board the bus. The girls had to assure the conductor that they would pay for the bus ticket and Ajay managed to get the whole group safely back to Kotdwar. This was not a normal incident. This shows his huge respect for the safety and security of women. Today the same is being reflected in the step that the Yogi administration has taken for the safety and security of all the women in Uttar Pradesh by deploying the Anti-Romeo squad.

Ajay chose ABVP over SFI

Ajay was always interested in politics and even in college chose to join student politics. His sister, Kaushalya, was married in Kotdwar and his sister's brother-in-law was in the Student's Federation of India (SFI), a left leaning student organization, connected with the Communist Party of India (Marxist). His brother-in-Law tried convincing Ajay to join student politics under SFI's banner. But Pramod Rawat (aka Tunna), convinced Ajay otherwise and made him join Akhil Bhartiya Vidyarthi Parishad (ABVP), the student wing of the RSS. After joining the ABVP, Ajay became very active on the field.

He was at the forefront of all the events, campaigns and protests organized by the ABVP in that region. Once, during a protest for Uttarakhand separation movement, Ajay faced a lathi charge by the police and saved a senior *karyakarta,* Rakesh Chamoli. The land of Kotdwar became the first teaching ground for Ajay for his social and political movements.

While talking about Ajay's Kotdwar days, his classmate Anil Bisht told that during the last year of college, one big ABVP workshop was conducted in Kotdwar where one outstation *karyakarta* (volunteer) was suffering from cholera and unfortunately died during the workshop. When no one came forth to handle the dead body and take it back to his hometown in Tadkeshwar, Ajay along with another volunteer took the initiative to personally ensure that deceased body was handed back to the family. In the process, Ajay also got seriously ill and had to be admitted in the hospital. The sense of responsibility and urge to help the needy was quite strong in Ajay since he was in college and now as Chief Minister of Uttar Pradesh, the urgency to improve people's life is evident in Yogi's actions.

How Ajay lost his first election in life

In 1992, Ajay wanted to contest for the secretary's position for the student body elections in his college. He could have got his candidature cleared from ABVP for the secretary position, but another student Padmesh Budlakoti from ABVP also asked for the ticket for the same position. To resolve the internal dispute, ABVP gave the ticket to a third person, Deep Prakash Bhatt. Ajay was a rebel even then. As he did not get the ABVP ticket, he contested the same position as an independent. Ajay lost the elections. Someone named Arun Tiwari won the secretary position in the Student Union of Government PG college of Kotdwar. Currently, Arun is an active member in Samajvadi Party and Padmesh Budlakoti is an active member of RSS in Kotdwar. This was Ajay Bisht's first election that he ever contested. After that he has not lost any elections till date. As Yogi Adityanath, Ajay fought five Lok Sabha elections, and won all of them.

Anil Bisht, Ajay's classmate while narrating the election incident told me that, during the election campaign preparation Ajay, slept over in a friend's room one night and the same night someone broke into Ajay's room and stole his certificates and documents, along with other things. This incident disturbed Ajay and he was not able to concentrate on elections to the fullest.

When Ajay's Parents met Yogi Adityanath, the Monk

After doing his graduation in Kotdwar, Ajay enrolled for Master of Science (MSc) in Mathematics in 1992 from Pandit Lalit Mohan Sharma Government PG College, Rishikesh. While he was in MSc first year, he started visiting Gorakhpur and meeting Mahant Avaidyanath. After a couple of meetings Ajay was convinced about joining Mahant Avaidyanath at the Gorakhnath Mutt as a full time disciple. In November 1993, Ajay left his village, his parents, his friends, and his studies and without disclosing much to anyone in the family, he went to Gorakhpur. On 15th of February1994, Ajay was anointed as a *Nath Panth yogi* by his *guru* Mahant Avaidyanath.

It was only after couple of months that Ajay's parents found out from the newspaper about his *sanyas*. Until then his parents thought that he had gone to Gorakhpur for some employment opportunity. After finding out, Ajay's parents reached Gorakhpur on the next available train and at the Mutt, Anand Singh Bisht, was shocked to see Ajay in a *sanyasi's* attire. Mahant Avaidyanath was out of station that time and Ajay had to calm his parents and made them talk to his *guru* on phone. Mahant Avaidyanath told Ajay's father that his son Ajay is Yogi Adityanath now. Mahant Avaidyanath further requested Anand Singh Bisht that of his four sons, one had decided to come with him for nation building and for strengthening Hinduism; and asked him to please allow him to serve the country. After initial resistance his parents gave in.

After couple of months Yogi Adityanath, came back to Panchur village, in Uttarakhand to take *Biksha* (alms) from his mother, as a part of the *Sanyasi* tradition. Since then

Ajay's parents have visited Yogi Adityanath in Gorakhnath Mutt couple of times. Now they call him "Maharaj ji', as others do, respecting the protocol and dignity of his role. Yogi Adityanath has also visited his hometown in Uttarakhand for a few important functions in the family. Yogi Adityanath has also established a college, Mahayogi Guru Gorkhnath College, near his village in Uttarkhand, under the Gorakhpur Mutt's administration.

Concluding the discussion with Ajay's parents I mentioned that hills of Uttarakhand have given Govind Ballabh Pant, Hemvati Nandan Bahuguna and Narayan Dutt Tiwari as Chief Ministers of Uttar Pradesh and now this house has given Yogi Adityanath as the fourth CM for Uttar Pradesh, hailing from the hills. To this, Savita Devi ji proudly recalled that Ajay always wanted to serve the people and now he is doing exactly that. With wet but contended eyes, Anand ji added that their lives are blessed as Ajay's parents and today they are proud of the monk who has become the Chief Minister of such a big state.